YOU'RE NOT REALLY HAMLET - AND EVERYBODY KNOWS IT

AN ACTOR'S HANDBOOK

To Jane!, thanks so much for your support and friendship all these years!

I hope you are well and that I get to see you sometime soon!

I hope you enjoy the book.

hugs,
Duane Daniels

Thanks to all the actors I have had the pleasure of working with. The students and actors at The Actor's WorkHouse, The Fritz Theatre, Space 55 and Buzzworks Theatre.

A very special thanks to Berridge Programs. To Andrea Mardon, who created the acting program and gave me space to develop these ideas, and to the staff there; Diarmaid, Greg, Emily, Brian, Bogdan, Kristy, Simon, Katie and Dan. And to the incredible acting students, who have contributed and inspired so much of this text. Thanks also to my trusted collaborator, Ron Foligno. And my Mom.

I am also grateful to my friends from The Fritz Theatre, where I began as an Artistic Director. Most notably, Karin, Bryan, Christina, Chris, Doug and Ed.

And thank you, Amy. For being my partner and best friend.

Duane Daniels

Illustrations: Matt Mays
Arrow Drawings: Duane Daniels
Cover Design: Sweet-Ass Merch
Cover Font: **LEMON/MILK** by Marsnev
© 2019 Duane Daniels

Introduction

Every actor is different. They (you) all come from different perspectives with different levels of experience. Acting is not one-size-fits-all.

I don't think actors are being told the truth. I think that the undefinable something is definable. A lot of people have it inherently. If you are one of those people this approach will help you understand exactly what it is you are already doing well. Exactly what those instincts are. If you don't naturally have these gifts, these techniques can help you adopt them.

I wanted to change that unreachable quality, that unattainable sense of you either "have it or you don't" - with this writing and with this theory — giving actors a practical approach to dramatic equations, an empowered approach to auditions, and to the stress of opening night.

What I hope to share is sort of an every day actor's point of view. This is what it's like for actors to work at it every day. It isn't magic. It's practical. And actionable.

When we see actors navigate this well, there are several terms we may choose to describe it. Often the word "talent" is used. There are others, but none of them are specific: "...that certain something... the it factor... charisma... sex appeal... star quality." Another popular phrase is taken from the French language: "Je ne sais quoi" which translated means "I don't know what."

In this book we will attempt to define these qualities. Each of these techniques are meant to empower you. To take a practical - yet powerful - approach to being an actor.

The Answer to Every Question

Isn't it helpful to have the answer to every question? And indeed, it is the answer to every question an actor might have. The question could be "how should I interpret the scene?" Or the question could be "should I cross right when I say this line?" Or the question could be "should I say this line loudly or softly?" "Pick up the glass in my left hand or my right hand?" There is one answer to all of these questions.

I said every question, and I meant it. "Should I pause here?" "Should I pick up the pace?" "Should I highlight this aspect of the character or that aspect of the character?" The answer is:

"Whatever will best serve the audience's experience."

That seems quite simplistic. It is. It doesn't provide us with any final answers, but lets us know which lens to look through.

Let's take note of the many things that are *not* the answer to every question. The answer to every question is not what makes sense, what we have experienced in the past, what is believable, or - by all means please - not what is logical.

We don't want to rule out what makes sense, what we have experienced, what is believable or what is logical. But those are not the answer to every question. The answer to every question is: Whatever will best serve the audience's experience.

This is something that is missing from most acting training. Most training is what we might call actor-centric. The techniques included in this book are audience-centric. The audience is the center of our universe, not the actor. The audience might be a theater filled with 200 people, the casting director sitting behind a desk, or a camera on set. Everything we do we will do with the audience's experience in mind.

After all, what are we hired to do? To present the material in a way that will reach and appeal to people who pay to see it. We are not hired to plumb our emotional depths or get in touch with our feelings so we can "really feel it." The audience's experience is the only one that matters. Ask any producer.

That doesn't mean that all of our training or emotional depth-plumbing won't help us in our work. To serve the audience's experience, it may be useful for the actor to get in touch with deep emotional feelings. It may be fitting to fearlessly portray anguish and grief, rage and jealousy. But it is important to remember that we do this to benefit our audience. Not so that we can indulge ourselves and our emotions, or to show everybody what a good actor we are. It's not about us.

We all want to be actors that give riveting performances. We need the audience for this. (Otherwise, who's being riveted?) We want to be compelling (for our audience) and memorable (audience again). In fact, nothing we do has merit unless the audience's experience is enhanced by it. Actors who best navigate these types of equations are the ones who give the most satisfying performances.

We do not exist in a vacuum. Our performances do not resonate without someone to receive them. It's basic physics. Give-and-take. Newton's Theory. For every action there is an equal and opposite reaction.

If we understand this idea - that it's our effect upon the audience that matters - we can begin to apply and make use of the basic principle that there is an equal and opposite reaction. By adjusting the choices that I make when playing a character, I am also changing the audience's experience.

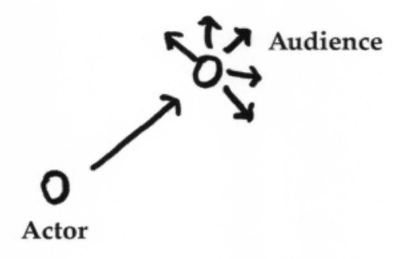

We have the opportunity to choose our actions based on those that cause the most desired reactions. When this equation is applied, greater power in our performances becomes definable.

With this approach, we will not try to plumb the depths of our own emotional despair, squeeze out all our tears or plunge ourselves dangerously into personal grief. This approach helps us understand what producers and directors already know: the audience is all that matters.

You're Not Really Hamlet, And Everybody Knows It.

It's kind of ridiculous really. You get the job of convincing everyone, and even yourself, that you are Hamlet. Then we give the audience a program that says, "Hamlet will be played by Steve Cooperstein. Steve lives with his dog Skooby and collects chicken feathers as a hobby." And now it's your job to not be Steve Cooperstein anymore. Now try to be Hamlet!

No one has ever become Hamlet. Thousands of actors have played the role - no doubt some of the best, but no one has become Hamlet. Not even once.

Hamlet is fictional. Many schools of acting say you should convince yourself that you are Hamlet. If the real Hamlet were on stage, he wouldn't know his lines or blocking. Talk about disempowerment! We've all been trying to do something which is fundamentally impossible. After all, you're you.

Imagine two actors in the same role. The same costumes, lighting, direction. The same basic physical appearance. Yet one actor may bring you to your feet in a standing ovation, and the other actor may leave you wishing you had stayed home. They're playing the same role!

What is one actor doing that makes the performance so compelling?

The Magic Trick

The Magic Trick is this: You are not an actor at all, you are the character you're playing.

In this moment, if I could make you in this classroom, casting office or theatre, forget that I'm an actor and instead believe that I am a peasant in Bolivia in 1862, wouldn't that be the greatest Magic Trick you've ever seen? Seriously.

INTRODUCTION

Forget making a quarter disappear, this is the real Magic Trick!

When you are an actor, you are a magician. When you're a magician, you are not fooled by your trick. That is the only way to be a good magician. You're there to give the performance, not be fooled by it. That's the audience's place in the equation. The Magic Trick works because they believe you're Hamlet. Not you.

Magicians don't believe in magic. Why? Because they know how it's done. They're not surprised when they pull a rabbit out of the hat. They put it there a half hour before the show.

So when we play Hamlet, (or any other role) it is not magic. There is no such thing as magic. Instead we are doing a Magic Trick. The job of the actor is to become a great magician.

Remind yourself in this process of the Ace of Clubs. This refers to that card up your sleeve. If the audience sees it, it ruins the trick. So when utilizing any of the techniques in this book, we want to do them powerfully and fully, but never let the audience see how we're doing the trick.

In order to not get caught, we'll sometimes stop doing (or even fail at) the trick for a moment. We can never let them catch us or be able to predict the outcome. So keep that Ace of Clubs you have up your sleeve (the trick, the technique) well hidden. If the audience sees it, that would be bad magic.

Before we get much further, I'd like you to consider this:

See what's possible, not what's there.

INTRODUCTION

If I could only give only one note to actors for the rest of my life - if I had to choose - it would be this one.

Most actors who audition for a role will see what's there. What's there is in the dialogue, the stage directions, the character description, the story. Seeing what's there isn't special. The best actors are those that discover the best possibilities for the character. What's possible, by definition, is not on the page.

The line of dialogue is just that: a line. Here is a drawing of a line:

\

Yep. it's a line alright. Very nice line you got there!

The line itself does not allow for nuance, repercussion or reverberation of the line. The line is merely the words we say. In itself, a line has no complexity. We can find opportunities to create reverberations around our line, repercussions to what we say.

As the actors cycle through in the audition setting and the casting people are making choices, they will be making decisions based on this equation, all other things being equal such as type, age, etc. The pages of the script have everything you say and everything you do. What the actor brings is an exploration and application of what's possible. Simply put:

The Best Actors Find The Best Possibilities.

CHAPTER 1:
ACTOR BRAIN / CHARACTER BRAIN

When performing, we are using both halves of our brain. One we'll call Actor Brain - which you already have because it's you. The other we'll call Character Brain - which we have to create.

First we will erase the notion that there is only Character Brain (Hamlet) Being an actor is to have a dual existence. There isn't only one thing going on - the character- it's the character and the actor. This book will help us figure out how Actor Brain and Character Brain work together. Then we can become fluid when using our two brains.

Actor Brain is you. The real you. The one standing there auditioning. The one hitting your mark. The one playing the laugh. Performing. Actor Brain is in charge of the preparation, the choices we will make in playing the role, and then in its execution. That's you up there. No matter what role you are playing. That is you up there playing it.

Character Brain is your character. The one in love. The one fighting hard for principles. The one striving and fighting and loving. Living. Character Brain is the illusion you create by actually having the character's thoughts, feelings and emotions right now, in real-time, while the audience watches.

Now that we understand that two brains are at work, we can begin to do the necessary task of creating the unified brain we can live in while performing. It's important to understand that Actor Brain is in charge. We'll need Actor Brain to navigate the performance. We will no longer try to pretend that it doesn't exist. We need it. Actor Brain was at rehearsal, Character Brain was not.

14

ACTOR BRAIN / CHARACTER BRAIN

Actor Brain is powerful. Because of its preparation, we can powerfully tell a story, inhabit a role, speak dialogue and execute blocking under the pressure and scrutiny of a performance. Actor Brain has developed instincts to present dynamic personas in complex emotional states.

Character Brain is off-balance. Even though it has firsthand Knowledge of its life, it cannot predict the future - or even the present. It is surprised by everything that happens next, including what it does or says. Character Brain has been trained to invest deeply in their life and to fight for their point of view.

When your two brains work well together, you'll be Powerfully Off-Balance. In this state, you'll give satisfying performances, and do it consistently. You (and those you work with) will be empowered to tell profound, compassionate stories and change the world. And that's exactly what you were meant to do. You're an actor.

We can understand the difference between actor thoughts and character thoughts, and how to create the best possible relationship between our two brains. During the process, when is Actor Brain in charge, and when is Character Brain in charge? And to what degree?

Think of it this way:

At the read-through, we'll be 90% Actor Brain - 10% Character Brain.

In performance, we'll be 90% Character Brain - 10% Actor Brain.

This is not the answer in all cases, or in all actors. But it's a nice ratio to examine. For many of us, it's a ratio to aspire to. While performing we will live as much as possible in

Character Brain, while using Actor Brain to navigate our performance.

Once we understand we are not Hamlet, we are now faced with a dilemma. The real Hamlet (if there was one) would have truth. Firsthand knowledge of his life and thoughts and fears. We - the actor - do not have this knowledge..

Actors are given a script. Their words are carefully chosen by playwrights and screenwriters. But saying them doesn't make them true. How can we bridge this gap? How can we create a new truth? First, let's identify where truth comes from.

In real life, who or what is writing our lines?

Exercise: Truth

Hey you! Reader! Yes you. Let's practice truth so we can get a diagram as to how it works. The character you are playing in this exercise is you, so there's no need for characterization or a script. Answer these questions truthfully and out loud. It may feel silly to talk out loud wherever you are. You can do it quietly if you want, but let's remember our basic questions: Where does the truth come from? Who or what writes my dialogue? It isn't important that what you recall is funny or smart or even interesting, only that it is true. You don't have to go into detail. No acting or improv please. Just tell the truth from your real life. Answer these questions truthfully. One at a time.

What did you do yesterday? (tell the truth from your real life)

Take note of your process you answer this. Where did you find your truth?

For most of us, the truth of an experience is in our video. Wherever we have been, whatever we hope for, we know what it looks like. This video is where we go to when telling the truth.

In the question above, you went to your mental videotape of yesterday. The truth of yesterday is in your images. If you stayed home and cleaned the house, perhaps you saw yourself with the vacuum and the cleanliness of your home when you were finished. Or maybe you went to work yesterday and your video is of you at your desk, or pulling in to your parking space and greeting a co-worker. Either way, the truth is in the video.

Here's another question. Again, just tell the truth.

Have you ever been to a high school prom?

For this answer, if you did go to a prom, you probably saw yourself dressed in what you wore. You saw the streamers and balloons. Maybe you saw the limousine you used to get there, or the corsage your date wore.

If you did not go to prom, your video might be of why not. You had to close at the burger joint where you worked or didn't care about going to prom. Either way, the truth is in the video.

Are you good at volleyball?

Your video - the visual history that plays like a movie in your brain - will be where you found your answer. If you said yes, the images in your video probably included you in athletic gear, making a perfect play on the volleyball, diving in the sand. If you said no, you probably saw yourself standing on the sidelines cheering at your friends playing, or the time you tried to play but discovered you had no talent for it.

Our personal movie - the video - will play in our brain and give us the information we need to then say "yes" or "no" truthfully.

Try these questions as well:

Are you a good cook?

Who is your favorite singer?

Have you ever traveled to another country?

When you answer truthfully, note your process. Your personal video comes to mind, and your words are in response to it.

To speak our dialogue truthfully, we will need to create a series of images to generate our character's language. We need to Shoot the Video.

Because actors have had rehearsal and someone gave them their dialogue, it is possible to say lines without video. But let's remember where the truth actually comes from: video first, words follow. This presents a blueprint for actors to create truth.

In order to speak truthfully, we must shoot the video on behalf of our characters during the rehearsal process so that when our characters are telling the truth, they will be referring to their own video. Their (our) first-person experience. Just as we identified our video in the exercise above about going to prom. The absence of this video is the absence of truth. Now that we have an understanding of truth as the process of video first and then words, we can go about creating truth for our characters.

This video is not limited to memories, (though that is a large part of video) but also includes fears, aspirations for the future, fantasies, secrets and whatever else our character's brain might see or imagine.

I asked you to speak out loud in the preceding chapter. Think of what you said as dialogue. If an actor was cast as you, how would they truthfully deliver the lines you spoke? Remember your prom video? In order to be truthful, the actor would need your video… or one as rich in detail.

When put into action, we can think of this as a game:

"This is my line of dialogue. What video do I need to shoot so I can *then* say this line truthfully?"

The video is also useful in memorization. If we can't remember our lines, it's because we haven't shot our detailed video. If we can't remember a word, our video is not specific enough. The more precise the dialogue, the more precise the video. Language - and gestures - are propelled forward, not because of our need to communicate our words, but our video.

Exercise: Shoot the Video

Shoot a video of "Aunt Martha." Take your time, perhaps you've known her your entire life. If that's true, you have memories at age five, fourteen, etc. Create those memories. Were you close? If so, you'll have to shoot those videos. If not, you'll need different ones.

Maybe the script indicates that "Aunt Martha" was a religious woman with a big purse. If that is so, you'll create videos to give you the experience of Aunt Martha, so that when you speak of her, you can say those lines truthfully.

Try this line of dialogue: "Aunt Martha was a lovely woman. I learned how to bake when I spent summers there as a kid."

Since all of the words in our dialogue need to be ours and not the writer's, we need video images to generate these words truthfully. Your character says she was "lovely." You might have chosen "good-looking" or "pretty" but you chose the word "lovely." The video for each of these words are specific to you. Whatever you identify as "lovely." It could be her clothes, hair, face, figure... Before you say the word "lovely," you may see a flower print dress. You see? "Lovely" isn't really "lovely" at all. It's a flower print dress.

"I" See yourself as younger.

"Learned." See your image of her teaching, you understanding, improving.

"How to." See a process, a sequence.

"Bake." See the oven, the mitts, the flour, the kitchen.

"When" See a period of time.

"I" You again.

"Spent" See time passing.

"Summers" Good weather, no school.

"There." See Aunt Martha's house, property, town.

"As a" See your image of transformation, change.

"Kid." You.

It isn't difficult. Shoot the video to a specific degree and you can move on. It probably won't take more than a minute. Then, when acting, use the "memories" you have created to generate your language. Now - using images first; words second - say the line truthfully.

"Aunt Martha was a lovely woman. I learned how to bake when I spent the summer there as a kid."

The best part is now that you have created truth, you don't have to pretend to have the truth. You don't have to "sell" anything. There is no need to convince an audience or camera. Nothing to fake. And you probably have the line "memorized."

There is another benefit to creating and implementing your video. In most cases, actors will feel an emotional involvement because they are confronted by the image. Aunt Martha may evoke feelings of nostalgia and warmth or may arouse feelings of fear and loneliness. This will be determined by what video you shoot. Either way, once we are confronted by the detailed video of Aunt Martha - even though she's fictional - she will inspire genuine emotional reactions.

Our audition session isn't directed. We don't get to be directed until after we're cast. When we take on the role of Self- Director, it becomes easier to get cast. It's easier because we come closer to bringing the director's vision to life. This can help us get more callbacks or (in the best- case scenario) the job.

Directors advocate for the audience. The director combines the material and the talent in order to have a profound effect. We can adopt the role of director in our own work and advocate for the audience. We don't have to wait for someone to do that for us. The techniques included in these pages assist us as self-directors.

Look at the casting process from the director's point of view. After seeing all the actors available, and narrowing the choices to the several people who read best for the role, at some point the director will say, "Everybody was good, but the one who is my choice is so and so." The director will select the actor who is already coming closest to the vision the director has for the script and the role.

Directors have a vision coming into the audition process and are looking for someone to fulfill that specific vision. If we take on the role of self-director, we will find ourselves and our interpretation of the role more closely aligned with their vision. It is commonly stated that "directing is 85% casting" or whatever number you might have heard. This is surprisingly true.

By becoming self-directors we give ourselves long term direction. We are identifying - and then sharpening - our instincts.

One of these instincts should be for our characters to have Knowledge (with a capital K)

If anyone said to you "you don't know what you're talking about!" You would probably be insulted. Yet actors (because someone else is telling them what to say - giving them their lines) often "don't know what they're talking about." For there to be any truth, we must have Knowledge (with a Capital K) of every word we say. Without paying attention to this fundamental idea, "you don't Know what you're talking about."

Just about anyone can say the words you were assigned to say. Speaking lines doesn't require any more knowledge than the average fifth grader. When we own the Knowledge of our language - the detailed video behind the words we say - we no longer have to pretend to know what we're talking about. The Magic Trick begins when you Know what you're talking about. Knowledge is power.

Imagine if the line speaks about your "sister." By definition, the word simply means a female from the same parents. The truth of the word is so many thousands of images - some good, some bad. When we have a truthful video, we understand the imperfection of the word.

Using our video and understanding its complexities also moves us past the limitations of saying the lines "good." Many actors can say the lines "good." In fact most anyone who calls themselves an actor, will be accomplished at line-saying. But our goal is higher. We can't let ourselves get

23

away with good line-saying. That is just so much yapping. Even when done well. The Knowledge is more complex than the words.

Our intention is to stop looking for the right way to say a line. There is no right way, and it would be boring anyway. Instead we recognize that since our words are imperfect, our communication is imperfect. Stop looking for the right way to say your line. The right way (What's There) is an answer. Answers are dead ends. Seeking and enjoying the wrong way (What's Possible) is more productive. The wrong way is full of possibilities.

When we Know what we're talking about - and make use of our character's video (images first, then words) we are creating a new truth. And that's an essential part of The Magic Trick.

Exercise: Naming Objects

Name out loud several objects, without first seeing a picture of them in your video. Go!

You were probably not able to name an object without seeing it first. For most of us, we see a picture, and a split second later we say the word "butterfly." Our brain sees an image and says "what's this called? Oh yes! 'Butterfly'" and then we say the word. It happens so quickly we barely notice.

Try this with naming your favorite foods or the cutest animals. To be truthful when acting, we'll need to follow this example. Images first, words follow.

The first part of the Magic Trick is that we're not actors at all. To become a good magician, we'll need to avoid doing things actors do.

Overall, actors will try to:

- Give the "Right" Line Reading
- Look Good
- Communicate Efficiently
- Be Believable
- Make Sense
- Keep Going

1.) Give the "Right" line reading

It's natural for actors to seek out the right line reading. After all, there may be producers or directors watching. We certainly want to impress our audience and make our characters convincing.

None of this is what a real person would do. They wouldn't seek out the right line reading because they don't have lines. There is no one watching them, so there's no one to convince.

2.) Look Good

It's natural that actors would want to look good. By definition, acting means being looked at. There has been a lot of effort put into costume and make-up.

In real life, people may be concerned about their appearance but not because of an audience or camera.

25

3.) Communicate Efficiently

Of course actors want to communicate efficiently. It seems that's what they are hired to do. There has certainly been lots of memorization and rehearsal.

But in real life, people don't communicate efficiently. We may be trying to, but our communication is quite flawed. We have never rehearsed so we don't know how to communicate efficiently.

4.) Be Believable

Naturally, actors want to be believable.

To try to make our characters believable means we are operating from an actor brain perspective. If we're concentrating on "make everybody believe me" then our objective is to be believable. Only an actor would have that objective. The Magic Trick is that we're not actors at all.

If we work mostly from the Character Brain perspective, our Actor Brain's need to be believable disappears. We don't have to try to be believable because we believe it ourselves. Our video is the proof of our truth.

The accountant doesn't go around trying to make everyone believe he's an accountant, he just is. The waiter doesn't need to go around convincing everyone they're a waiter, because they really are one. By trying to convince everyone, you are automatically defining the experience as untrue.

Only someone who is not a waiter would try to convince others that they *are* a waiter. If you are trying to be believable, you are fighting for the actor (yourself) and not the character. Our goal is to fight harder for our characters than we are fighting for ourselves.

5.) Make Sense

If it all makes sense, why is the audience watching? If everything is logical, why are they there? They can see logic everywhere, They already know where logic will lead them. So when you get there, they'll be waiting for you wishing they had their two hours back.

6.) Keep Going

Actors know there is more to the scene, that their monologue has 2 more paragraphs. They know their next line and the one after that.

But in real life, we don't have that "keep going" outlook. We have no idea how many more lines we have or when the scene will end. In fact it never ends. So we don't keep going. We even stop sometimes.

In the Anti-Acting section of this book, we will address these tendencies and find an empowered relationship to them.

Anti-Acting (Breaking the Rules)

Acting is not like real life. Real people are not given their dialogue and don't memorize their lines. The Magic Trick requires that the audience not see our preparation, our memorization. We can begin by recognizing the inherent untruth of words.

Too often, actors like to think that the words are what is true for their characters. However in life our words are just our words. The truth (video) for our characters is very different from the things they say.

"Love" is just a word. In itself, it is not an emotion. It is just the word we use for it. A placeholder.

Take the word "school." Schools have campuses and parties, students and football games. The word school is not the experience of school. It is simply a word. The truth of "school" has much more detail than the word could ever provide. Using video and possibilities we can embrace its deeper and more complex meanings.

When our character says school, let's not mean a big building where students gather. Instead our thoughts might be, "I was so popular!" while we are saying the word school. This concept embraces the imperfection of the word. It doesn't try to distill or even define it. Our approach embraces that school means many things. Our job as actors is to explore those many things. The possibilities.

If the word we are referring to is "restaurant," we will explore ideas removed from the word restaurant. Perhaps the bad service you got there and the color of the napkins or the great meal on your first date with your spouse.

Earlier, when you were asked if you had gone to prom your truthful experience may have looked like this:

You were asked a question. Needed truth. Went to brain filing system. Searched. Opened files. Searched. Found video file. Opened video file. Searched. Found many videos. Assessed videos. Came to conclusions. Spoke.

If you responded truthfully saying the word no, your videos may have been the part-time job you had to work and that you couldn't afford a tuxedo. Or that you couldn't get a date, and you did something else that was more fun anyway. Then you said "No."

If you responded truthfully saying the word yes, your videos may have been the corsage you wore and how proud your mom looked, or that it wasn't as fun as you thought and that Johnny Wilson puked. Then you said "Yes."

Is it true that you *did not* go to prom? Yes. How do we know it's true? "My boss at the fast food place was a jerk."

Is it true that you *did* go to prom? Yes. How do we know it's true? "Johnny Wilson puked."

The truth of the word "yes" is not within the word "yes" at all. Why would we want it to be? That would be boring. We may have been excluding the truth and all the opportunities it presents by trying to play the game correctly and within the boundaries of the "good "line reading. It's like trying to be sincere by saying to yourself "look sincere! look sincere!" By pretending to have the truth we may be excluding the real thing.

If you truthfully said no or yes - that one word of dialogue - so many images were needed to discover and then communicate that truth. All of them were surrounding the word, not within it.

The human mind is curious. Curious to discover threats, sexual innuendo. We don't live in a state of knowing, but a state of not knowing.

In life how many thoughts do we have per minute? According to the Laboratory of Neuro Imaging at the University of Southern California, the average person has about 48.6 thoughts per minute. That adds up to a total of 47,000 thoughts per day.

It would be impossible for us to articulate the details of every one of those thoughts. Each individual image can have hundreds of details. When we say "prom," we don't take the time to mention what color the balloons were but they are in the video. If you are focused on the color of the balloons, you don't have time to talk about how many there were. Nor would you choose to - the balloons aren't the point. But they are part of the truth.

As a truthful video of prom plays in your head, you will see the balloons even though you don't mention them. They aren't what you are trying to express. But in your video, they are there. So perhaps, are the banners or the school colors. The word we are saying ("prom") is true because of what we are not saying.

According to a study by Psychologist Matthias Mehl of The University of Arizona, the average person speaks about 16,000 words per day. That means we have three thoughts for every word. Even if one of the thoughts is directly related to the word we're saying, by the time we finish saying it, we've had at least one other thought. When we consider how many thoughts go through our minds but do not become language, it's kind of mind-boggling. A new thought virtually every second. A constant state of discovery. Living life is to be in a constant state of surprise.

In real life, all of us are living in a state of surprise all the time. As you read this, if your phone rings or a car horn honks outside, it surprises you. As I sit in class, I'm surprised by everything, whether a student nods off, coughs or scratches their knee.

In real life, we don't know what our lines are, or how to say them. We haven't read the script. We don't know how this scene is going to play out. We haven't learned our dialogue. We weren't at rehearsal.

An actor has had rehearsal, so there are no surprises. Everything has been carefully laid out so that nothing can go wrong. How do we overcome the fact that we know everything that's going to happen? By changing our minds, Abruptly and Often.

To change our minds abruptly and often resembles real life; that new thought almost every second. When acting, as soon as we "know" what we're feeling, what we're thinking, move to the next thought. Explore further. Stay curious.

In life we are constantly learning and taking in new information. Our brains are like a computer that is always downloading. Each piece of information we take in adds to our knowledge of our situation and surroundings. These updates happen so quickly that we don't have time to observe them. Our lives are always streaming. By changing our minds abruptly and often when acting, we can simulate this state of surprise.

In our technique, if we force our character brain to change its mind, it doesn't allow us to know what's next. We understand that our lives are moving forward, there is always another question.

Now in real-time, when we decide to change our minds, we will have to decide "to what?" Answering this question forces us to re-examine our video, confront the lives of our characters and swim deeper.

This is the perfect marriage of Actor and Character Brain. Actor Brain executes dialogue and blocking while Character Brain lives in the state of surprise.

The state of surprise helps us create the illusion that we have never been here or experienced this before. It erases the rehearsal. It erases the director. It can even erase the actor so that what we're left with is the character. At least, that's the illusion.

In an attempt to do a good job and keep things moving, actors may find themselves swimming fast. Swimming fast skims the surface of the water. To swim deep is to embrace the depths and complexities of our characters.

It is uncomfortable down there. There is no air. It's scary as hell. When we fight hard for our characters we see that our characters don't get to stop living their lives when the scene ends. They are still deep in the waters of their lives. If we swim deep with them, we can understand the depths and complexities of our character's realities.

Take the audience down there with you. If we swim deep and take the audience with us, we can force them to confront our character's situation even though it is harshly uncomfortable. Of course we have to let them up for air once in a while or they'll drown, but don't let them stay above the surface of the water too long. Take them back under.

Slowing down our rate of speech can help. Actor Motor often gives us an artificially fast pace in our language. If we dial back Actor Motor, we can confront our character's plight. And give the audience the opportunity to confront it also.

Actor Motor is that part in our brain that's wound very tightly. Most of us need to be aware of our actor motor and get it under control. The Actor Motor won't let you settle in. It has to keep driving forward. It spins at a high rate and squeaks in a high pitched voice, "Keep going, keep going! They're watching!" We move at an artificially quick pace. There's no time for your character to reflect. There's no time for your character to consider anything.

We want to turn down our Actor Motor. It's like turning down the revs on the carburetor in an old car. If we can do that, we give ourselves time to swim deep in the character.

Actor Motor is understandable. It's high stakes to get up there; in class, at an audition, on camera. It's a natural reaction for our actor motor to spin at a high speed. But the magic trick is that we're not actors at all. If we fall victim to our Actor Motors, we are not being good magicians.

Actor Motor also manifests itself physically. Actors will lean forward – a tendency to lean toward a fetal position - which is a safe feeling, but detracts from the ability to invite the audience in. Actor Motor can also lead to overacting, which is not a phrase we use often, but this is where overacting would originate. Actor Motor can cause us to "sell" the lines or characters or ourselves.

"Do a good job! Do a good job!" is part of the Actor Motor, too. When we can really make sure that we get the "do a good job" motor (Actor Brain) out of our work, it will give us room to fight harder for our characters.

Actor Motor prevents us from being in character brain. We don't have time to live in that moment, experiencing the character's experiences. An Actor Motor at high speed is rushing us to the end of the scene, play or day of shooting. If we get it dialed back, we can fight harder on behalf of our characters.

Patience is one of the hardest things for actors to learn. It's challenging (and takes a great deal of courage) to give ourselves permission to play a role where we don't have it all figured out. But let's live powerfully in the uncertainty of our character's existence, in real time, right now. Take the risk of being surprised.

It is usually not till we get way down underneath the surface, that we discover what is possible. Once we are down there and actually confront our character's circumstances, we will find opportunities we could not have predicted. We may even find some involuntary emotional reactions.

We want to confront the realities of our character. The character doesn't only exist for the three minutes of the scene. They continue to fight long after that last line. To Swim Deep is to fully confront our character's world.

This brings us to the concept of Arrows. Arrows are a tool we'll use many times throughout this book.

Arrows show us how to move away from the line of dialogue. They create space between our words and our thoughts, like real life. They give the audience (and actor) space to explore and make discoveries. Arrows lead us away from the line (the answer) and into possibilities. They give us an emotional playing field.

Below, we also will use arrows and look into how they can help us in producing tension.

The arrows above indicate flow. They are predictable. Comfortable. They can cause the audience to tune out, their ears to fall asleep. Emotionally, it is uneventful. Everything falls logically, step by step, towards a predictable conclusion. There is no element of surprise here. So...

Instead...

Think of each arrow as a line of dialogue. This concept is not limited to lines of dialogue, but let's start there. The preceding drawing is telling us, "Don't let line A and line B mean the same thing." In fact it is the contrast between the 2 lines (A and B) that makes each line more powerful.

Line B becomes more powerful because it is contrasted with Line A.

When we use opposing arrows between line A and line B, We are going from here, to here, emotionally. Line B becomes an event, not another line of dialogue. Something happened instead of something being said. Audiences would rather witness events than hear dialogue. Line B is now an event.

If we supply greater contrast between Line A and Line B, we can cause a larger event.

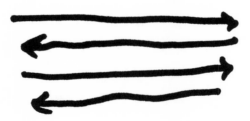

The story of a line A is enhanced because of the contrast we employ with line B. Line B becomes more powerful because it is contrasted with Line C. The power of each line is enhanced because it contrasts with the line preceding it, and again with the one that comes after it. Each line means something markedly different and distinct. Our dialogue is full of events, not just talking.

Contrast tells a powerful story

We can use arrows to lead us away from what's "there" and help us discover "what's possible."

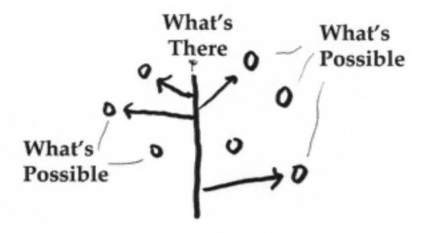

What's "there" is:
the line
the scene
the words

So let's use arrows to move us away from the line, the scene and the words.

Exercise:

While saying "Don't leave me Margaret, I love you."
One at a time, think:"What will I do without you?"
"If you're going, GO"
"I'll get by somehow."
"Give me one last chance."
"How dare you betray me."

Each of these points of view will give you a different "reading" of the line and will affect the audience's experience. We can then look for the choices that will affect the audience most profoundly.

There isn't a right or wrong answer for the above. The strongest choices would depend on the other aspects of the story, the specifics of the scene and even the actor making the choice. The possibilities are nuanced and virtually unlimited. But to give the most satisfying performances, we'll need to explore these possibilities and come up with the most powerful juxtaposition of these two ideas. One being the line and the other, the thought.

Try the same line with these "readings:"
"You can't resist me!"
"This is your last chance!"
"I've said this a million times."
"Love is painful."
"Finally!"

There are also occasions when you might say the line with this "reading."

"Don't leave me Margaret, I love you." This reading is what we call a "succeed moment." (See Inviting Failure)

Also, try the line using various emotional values. The line looks like it should be said sadly or pleadingly. See what happens when you avoid the logical choice.

In these pages we don't talk much about motivation or subtext. That's because asking the question "What's my motivation?" is bad magic. Only an actor would ask that question. The character wouldn't. If we're asking that question we're defining ourselves as the actor, not the character. If your character is at a job interview with a hungry child at home, we don't need to ask "What's my motivation?" The video already has the answers.

Think what the character thinks. See what the character sees. And remember what the character remembers. Right now. In real-time.

When we have a first-person video for our character, we know what our motivation is. The first person video (point of view) has all of that information without the self-consciousness of having to ask the questions in the first place.

The way many of us have been trained to act is to try to look as if you think what the character thinks, try to convince us you can see what the character sees, and to be believable when acting like you remember what the character remembers. This is faking the truth. Why fake truth when we can create it? The truth is in our video, our first-person point of view. All we have to do is shoot the appropriate video. Then it will be easier to think what the character thinks, see what the character sees and remember what the character remembers.

If we can think, see and remember as the character thinks, sees and remembers, we can live truthfully while the audience (or camera) watches. We are living in character brain; the first person thoughts of the character. After all, isn't that the illusion?

Acting is pretend. It's your imagination and craft that are giving you the circumstances of the character. On the stage, in the classroom or on the film set, none of it is real. Actors rightfully want to create the illusion however, that it is.

When we shoot the video for our character, now we have to decide what the video(s) should be. "Which real?"

Simply being real doesn't make our work interesting. We can see real everywhere. We can look in the window at a laundromat and see people really doing their laundry. Nothing could be more real than that. All around us we can see people being real. Accountants are really adding numbers, mechanics are really fixing cars and housekeepers are really vacuuming, but an audience wouldn't pay to watch.

Having a video is not enough. The mere fact that it is "truth" doesn't make it important or relevant or even interesting.

To be real is part of our objective, but it is not the objective. It is not enough to create something real and be done with it. Instead we will craft our video in such a way as to most affect the audience. We have to find the most dynamic dramatic equation.

So the question of "which real?" becomes: "How do we craft our video in order to create the best possible experience for our audience?"

To stand on stage, or in front of the camera, would be the scariest thing imaginable to some people. For us to rise to these occasions is very similar to the athlete rising to the top of their game. There isn't room for timidness, apologies or fear. We are fighting for our characters.

We want to "take the audience on an adventure" or to "take the audience on a journey." Look at the operative word here: "Take." Many of us consider the action of taking as impolite. It is. In fact, no riveting performance can be done "politely."

Audiences are moved because they are confronted. What they discover there helps them look at their lives in a new light because they have been transported to another time and place. They won't go on their own. We have to take them.

It's important to remember that we use these techniques in order to take loving care of our audiences. We do it on

41

ACTOR BRAIN / CHARACTER BRAIN

their behalf. The journey we will take our audience on is uncomfortable at times. The powerful story is never the polite one.

In the relationship between actor and audience, the audience has agreed that the actor will be in charge. After all, that's why they are all facing one direction and the actor is alone facing the other. In a 500 seat theater with one performer on stage, that's a thousand eyes to the actor's two. It is necessary for the actor to take a dominant position.

We want to make something happen. Not to *allow* it to happen, or to *hope* it happens, but to make it happen. We are not there to be observed. We are there to create emotional action.

When an audience attends your production (or tunes in to your TV show or movie) they are agreeing to (and actually seeking out) the experience of being led. We can't lead tentatively. The audience has tuned in to your performance in order to experience something. Not to observe something. The audience watching a performance, but not invested in the experience, is not receiving a powerful story.

Without this Aggressive Act, the audience is comfortable. If the audience is comfortable, we are not communicating powerfully. For every action there is an equal and opposite reaction, right? But without an action, there is no reaction.

An excellent study* discovered that the profession with the most testosterone is... acting. Not the professions that might be considered macho (including, in this study, football players and firefighters), but acting.

*Heroes, Rogues, and Lovers: Testosterone and Behavior. James McBride Dabbs, Mary Godwin Dabbs (Authors)

Since acting is the profession with the most testosterone, it stands to reason that to be a professional actor, we will have to nurture ours.

As with most of our techniques I'll remind us of the **Ace of Clubs** on Aggressive Act. It will not serve our audience's interest if they see us being aggressive. However it does serve the audience's interest to make something happen.

For every action (you, story) there is an equal and opposite reaction (audience)

For our purposes in Newton's theory, we will define the Aggressive Act as the action that will then cause in the audience an emotional reaction. It initiates the flow between story and audience. Causes movement. Causes our audience to be "moved."

Without Aggressive Act   **With Aggressive Act**

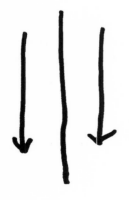

43

ACTOR BRAIN / CHARACTER BRAIN

A lot of actors will ask "How should I say this line?" Some actors look in the mirror and practice faces that represent emotions.

I do not recommend these methods. We don't want to know how to say the line. That is disingenuous to the character. We don't want to know what face we make for the same reason.

Instead of showing what the face might have shown as we rehearsed in the mirror, (Outside-In) very strongly identify that emotion within yourself, feel it, exploit it and then allow it to be seen on your face (Inside-Out). If the emotional value is high enough and you allow it to be seen, you don't have to "show" anything.

The same thing is true of gestures. Actors may ask, "Should I raise my arm when I say this line?" Again, if raising the arm tells the story, let it happen on its own, because you're powerfully connected with telling that story. If the arm raises, it raises. If it doesn't you didn't need it in the first place.

Outside-in is Actor Brain trying to look convincing, concerned with what your face and hands are doing. Inside-out is preferable. That's where we can find Character Brain. The face, hands and gestures do what they do because we're seeing our video and feeling the emotions that result. The preferred process is from the inside-out.

44

We want to be fighting harder for our characters than we are for ourselves. This requires us to be inside-out. Inside-out doesn't have judgment or plans about what to do in the moment. It lives with the point of view of the character without the need for vanity or representation in our performance.

Always remember to mitigate everything with the ace of clubs. None of what we are talking about is 100 percent true. All the rules can be broken or used in percentages. Dance or clowning would be a combination of outside-in and inside-out.

There are other uses for outside-in. Physical comedy would be one. We might know that a certain angle or body language will enhance a moment. In those cases, we would pre-plan our actions. My hero, Dick Van Dyke, did it in rehearsal over and over again – each movement worked out. The trick is to then live in Character Brain while executing those physical moves.

When you're given a specific piece of blocking such as hit a certain mark, for a period of time this will be in our Actor Brain as we rehearse our steps in to the scene. Our technique might tell us to rehearse the steps backwards, too. The job now, is to take that physical Actor Brain task and turn it into a Character Brain behavior.

A powerful performance is when the audience leaves different than when they came in. They are inspired to do better. To become better husbands or wives, better friends, a better dad or mom, a better boss, a better partner, more charming. But audiences won't be moved unless we move them. To do this, we can use Impolite Story.

Think back to the movies and plays you've seen. Your all-time favorites, whatever they are. Your own list of best performances.

These stories and performances affected and inspired you. They are examples of great heroism and sacrifice. Large obstacles were overcome. You were moved. And none of it was done politely.

Stories have impact because of impoliteness. In The Wizard of Oz - something we think of as entertainment for children - the impoliteness is everywhere: the tornado that sweeps away a young girl, the meanest witch imaginable, setting a man of straw on fire, flying attack monkeys, the wicked witch's melting flesh...

It is because of this impoliteness that the images and story stay with us for a lifetime. Because the characters are so severely unreasonable, there is a greater release when these obstacles are overcome. The more impolite the story, the greater the consequences. To make the story more impolite is to make it more important.

In the heart-warming film "It's a Wonderful Life," the story of redemption is so great because the lead character is suicidal. The powerful story of love and family is told in contrast to the impoliteness of suicide and remorse. If the suicide and remorse were more polite, such as "Oops and I'll try to do better next time." no one would remember the movie.

Mr. Potter (in the same movie) represents greed and vindictiveness. Not politely, but so impolitely as to virtually set the standard when it comes to portraying these qualities. The willingness of each actor to let us see their ugliness, their desperation, shows us how impoliteness works. When

46

looked at in this light, one of the most beloved films of all time is actually about self-loathing and malevolence.

Why would audiences all gather together and pay money to watch average things happen? Why would they all agree to be silent and pay close attention if what's going to take place is going to be mundane and regular? They don't. They gather together for the impolite story.

This impoliteness isn't necessarily in our characters. It isn't simply finding ways for our character to be rude. It is in our (Actor Brain) willingness to take the audience to uncomfortable places.

In our real lives, we don't force people to confront loneliness, fear, loss, failure. It isn't socially acceptable. It wouldn't be polite. But when it's time to take the audience, to create a meaningful and vivid experience, it's time to be as impolite as possible. As impolite as we can conceive of, and then a bit more. Through these difficult ideas, we can "raise the stakes" for our characters.

Most of us don't go around making people uncomfortable all day long. We probably say "thanks" and "have a nice day" when interacting with strangers. When performing, get rid of politeness, so that we can have as much impact as possible. As actors, we provide examples for our audience. It is up to us to present powerful ones.

When Sherlock Holmes-ing your script, assume the story to be as impolite as possible. Don't let this approach make everyone secret murderers, just raise the stakes. Make the consequences greater. As long as we apply this idea without getting caught by the audience or camera (Ace of Clubs) we are heightening the impact of our work.

In auditions, actors are usually given a page or two and don't know the overall arc of the characters. We also may not have a clue about the story. This can be very disempowering. Let's use impolite story to get some power back.

Actors will typically look at a scene and come to reasonable conclusions. But when we discover the full story - the other seventy pages of the script - we're surprised at how much more impolite the story is than we had thought.

Imagine auditioning for Paula Vogel's "How I Learned to Drive" or Edward Albee's "The Goat" without knowing the full story. You might assume they are about driving lessons or someone's pet. They're not.

Impoliteness raises the stakes in comedy too. Think of "The Nerd" by Larry Shue or "See How They Run" by Philip King or even "As You Like It" by Shakespeare.

Not only do we want to tell an impolite story, we want to tell it impolite-ly. We are toying with them emotionally, setting them up to feel something, manipulating their emotional responses. It would be rude to do this anywhere else. When acting, embrace this impoliteness.

Powerful storytelling is an emotional gut-punch. When audiences experience an emotional gut-punch, they appreciate the experience. It is satisfying, perhaps even profound. Whether it is comedy or drama, the emotional gut-punch is why people see films and go to the theatre.

Whether it's comedy or drama, any genre, to have the audience care about what happens next - to have them invest in our story - requires tension. If there's no tension, why would they care? They don't. Without tension the audience is relaxed in their chairs and thinking about what they have to do tomorrow.

Let's assertively initiate flow with the audience. We can't wait for this flow to occur, or hope it occurs. We must reach across the chasm between us. Make something happen.

Tension is what makes a scary movie scary and a funny movie funny. Tension is why the audience laughs, cries, screams, or cheers. It makes the audience a participant in our story instead of just an observer.

Tension helps them become invested in our character's life. They hope your character gets the job, or you win over the love of your life. The more they hope - the more tension - the more satisfying their experience.

When we recognize there are two points - actor (or story) and audience - there is an opportunity to activate those two points, so that there is an energy moving between them. There's a relationship. A flow. One point cannot have tension. It takes two for there to be a reaction to our action. Our job is to impact that second point in a way that productively and powerfully communicates our story.

We have a relationship and a responsibility toward that thing out there. That's not nobody, we're not alone, we're not in a vacuum. It's like a radio signal. so our job is to have an effect upon that thing that is hearing our radio signal, watching us perform. Our job is to make sure that the relationship is vibrant and active like an electrical current.

If a tree falls in the forest, and no one hears it, does it make a sound? What we're suggesting is, no it doesn't. (Scientifically it makes a sound but dramatically it does not) It is the act of hearing that creates the sound, the someone who hears the sound is our audience. When we include the audience in our work, we're plugging in to the electricity and providing a current to turn our audience on. With no one to hear the tree fall, there is no sound. Look at this metaphor - suddenly our work becomes an equation.

We can utilize flow and the interruption of flow. Think of expectation - which is a tendency in one direction - and surprise, a sudden change in the other direction.

We can also find tension in the juxtaposition of ideas. If the line of dialogue is "Go" and the meaning behind our word is "stay," we are creating tension between two points with one word. The audience is left to wonder what's really going on. It gives them space to investigate. We have spoken only one word but created tension between two points; what we say and what we think.

The Opposing Ideas of our line of dialogue and the meaning behind it might not be completely opposite. If our line of dialogue is "Go" and the meaning behind our word is "I'll get by somehow," we are still giving the audience space to explore. The actor is creating tension for the question of whether or not we will indeed "get by." We're giving the audience two points: Our word "Go" and our inner thought. The word we say has a counter-idea against which it can resonate. We are conveying twice as much information. Not only what we're saying, but what we're not saying.

Tension is not sustainable indefinitely. The balloon can burst. We can also use release. This is what causes the audience to laugh or have an "Aha" moment. Tension creates an expectation, and the audience gets their reward at the release.

Don't Let What You Say Dictate How You Say It

Words are definitely not truth, so to say them "good" is deadly. The correct reading has no resonance. No repercussions, just the line. It is in opposition to the line that our words resonate.

This diversion between the lines and our intentions, gives the audience a place to explore. It invites them in and provides questions so they can take an interest in our character's life. It is more valuable to provide questions for our audience then it is to provide answers. Audiences would rather come to their own conclusions. We save the answers for the last page of our story. In the moment-to-moment world of our characters, provide plenty of questions for our audience to investigate. This gives them a reason to stay tuned, come back for act two, or look forward to next week's episode.

The words themselves are already doing the dramatic action *of* the words, so we don't need to do that. That's already there. What we're bringing to the words is opposition, texture, nuance, consequence. All of that is opposed to the words on the page. If we do the line "right" we won't discover which awesome ways there are to do it wrong.

To say the line "I love you" lovingly is simply redundant. It is in an opposing idea "I love you" - as a warning for example - that we can find dynamic dramatic opportunities. Or the line "I love you" as a reminder. Again, what is dramatically interesting is away from the words, not within them.

Secondly, do words convey feeling, or do they merely attempt to? In the line "I love you," do those words adequately describe my characters feelings? Shall I reduce my feelings to fit within those four letters? Is the truth really within those four letters? No. They are just typing. Four letters masquerading as a feeling, but not a feeling.

We can "love" our parents, our goldfish, our favorite slippers and hamburgers. The actual feelings we have toward these things vary greatly. The word "Love" doesn't really mean anything. The word is only a word.

Words are most certainly not truth in themselves. They are the distillation of truth. The runoff. The residue. We use so many words because none of them are quite right. Words merely encircle the truth of what we are trying to communicate. They are an attempt to describe the truth. Not truth itself.

An actor's response to a line of dialogue might be to say to themselves,"My job is to make these words true." No. We diminish the truth by trying to make it fit within the words of dialogue. Truth is much more complex than words could ever be.

Even words which are spoken sincerely and honestly do not contain (all of) the truth. This leads to an interesting question:

How do we say our lines truthfully?

We don't look for the truth inside of the line. The truth is outside of the line. In the point of view and details that are not spoken.

If it Feels Good, Don't Do it

A lot of actors wonder what it is to over-act. It is when it feels good, and then we do it. We shouldn't indulge ourselves in our emotions. In the moment when our Actor Brain identifies that it is feeling good, we must change our mind, so that we don't continue to indulge. We have to throw ourselves back into a state of not knowing.

When we are performing, our Actor Brain may have an impulse such as "Wow I'm really good at this emotion!" or "I'm really nailing this scene!" or "if I say it like this, it will be perfect!" In these moments avoid indulgence.

If you are aware you are kicking ass, you are in your Actor Brain. Dive back into Character Brain. Your character hasn't had rehearsal. If you are kicking ass - that is, it feels good and you do it - the audience will see the actor at work.

The character you are playing is not concerned with playing the character you are playing. You shouldn't be either. If we are to succeed at the Magic Trick that we are not actors, it would not serve us to get caught giving a great performance. That would ruin the illusion that it isn't a performance at all.

If I am willing to avoid indulging in my performance, another benefit arises. Instead of highlighting how wonderful an actor I am, I can give that power to the story and the writer. To not allow yourself to do that thing that would feel good (indulge yourself emotionally, deliver the line perfectly, etc.) will throw you back into a state of surprise.

Like many of the ideas in this book, If it Feels Good Don't Do it is inviting the actor to present the other side of each coin. It helps the audience to consider the story and

53

characters and situations in a complex way. We are reminding our audience that everything is not always what it seems, that there is more to the story than meets the eye. More than simply the things being said.

*"The only way I **cannot** say my line is **the way I know I am going to**."*

When you practice and apply this technique, you are forcing yourself to change your mind. Often. Maybe even 48.6 times per minute. You keep yourself in a state of surprise.

Maybe you have had the experience of seeing a performance that causes a room to go silent. That you-can-hear-a–pin-drop moment.

We are trying to create those moments where you could hear a pin drop. In fact a series of pin-drop moments. Creating discomfort is our avenue toward a pin-drop moment.

Picture yourself as the actor in the waiting room at an audition. The assistant running the audition comes to the waiting room and says your name. As you rise to enter the room I advise you to have a series of thoughts:

"Before I worry about saying my lines well, or making a good impression, or God forbid Acting Good, I'm going to make sure of one thing. And that is to create discomfort through my work."

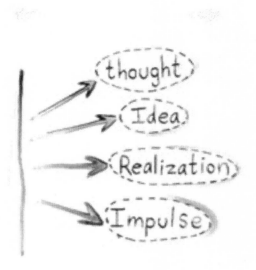

Even such basic ideas as charm or charisma, humor and sex appeal, all inherently have tension as a requirement. Without tension our audience (in this example the casting team) will not be engaged in our work. Let's aggressively seek the idea of discomfort, because without it the audience does not even need to pay attention. Discomfort is what causes our audience to want to know what happens next, to root for our character, and not be able to take their eyes off of our performance.

Inviting Failure

Many actors can say the lines "good." This in itself, is not an effective Magic Trick. Of course actors can say the lines "good." Given the advantage of rehearsal and study time, actors will begin to succeed more and more in their communication. There will be fewer missteps. They will become more efficient. Their goal will be for the character's communication to be successful. More and more they will mean exactly what they say.

But words are not thoughts and thoughts are not words. In real life, our communication is quite flawed. People don't only mean what they say. They mean many other things, and they often mean them more than the things they are saying.

Inviting Failure gives us the freedom to create spontaneity, texture, consequence, resonance, nuance, etc. Failure is what the lines resound against. If we succeed or sell the lines, we have nothing to resonate against. Failure is what gives the line of dialog context.

What we're identifying here is to try to stop saying the lines "right." It makes perfect sense to say the lines right when you're an actor. After all we've had lots of rehearsal and memorization. We have figured everything out. And it feels that our job is to say all of the lines right.

What happens when we embrace doing it "wrong?" Not having it all figured out but live our (character's) life anyway. We add texture and nuance to our dialogue. We help reveal the humanity in our characters. We create tension and room for exploration for our audience. And we help to show the experience of what we're talking about, not merely the facts. Inviting failure helps us to navigate our character's waters because we are accepting them as choppy and that we do not control our ocean.

Inviting failure is to recognize the ocean for its power, not pretend we can control it. We are not navigating our waters if we are in control of the ocean. To pretend we can control our ocean would be as pointless as surfing on a parking lot.

We don't always fail. Sometimes we can succeed. Use "succeed" moments to make your character's most powerful points. We often illustrate a succeed moment as when our head, heart and gut are all in alignment; as in the line: "Don't go!"

By succeeding in a line like this, we are telling a powerful story. The contrast between failing and succeeding lets the audience in on what is most important to our characters. Not everything we say is equally important. By adopting this fail/succeed technique, we carve a powerful path for our story.

Unreasonableness

The audience did not come here to see you behave reasonably. Dramatic power lies in what is unreasonable. It follows then, that we might avoid what is reasonable.

The television show The Office is a great example of unreasonableness. If the character of Dwight can't find his stapler, it is his unreasonableness that gives us dramatic, or in this case comedic, action. If he were reasonable about a missing stapler, not only would it be a less interesting moment dramatically, we basically wouldn't have the character at all. The character himself is based on unreasonableness; —unreasonably convinced of this, unreasonably attracted to that. Unreasonableness creates large dramatic action.

If you or I in real life were to lose our stapler, we would reasonably set about finding it, or borrowing one from a co-worker. We're good people and behave reasonably. But no-one would tune in to watch you as your average, reasonable self. If there's nothing unreasonable happening, there's very little to see.

How may we apply this idea? If we play a character who is attracted to our therapist, dramatically it is important to be unreasonably attracted to her. If we want the job, we want the job to an unreasonable degree. If our character dreams of playing the cello, let's dream in an unreasonable way. The audience does not want to watch reasonable things happen. Unreasonableness helps us avoid the average, the neutral, the vanilla. It also aids us in discovering what is possible, not what is there.

I'll put this in the context of an audition situation, but it's true across the board. In the audition process, if they see 100 people for the role, be one of the ten best or ten worst, don't be the middle 80. When I say this in class, sometimes a student asks "What do you mean by worst? Do you mean just do anything crazy?"

The eighty actors in the middle will not be remembered. They will be the actors that made the average, safe choices. Those actors made choices based on things like logic. They did what makes sense. They tried to fit within the limitations of the logic of their lines. They are trying to do what will please the casting team, of doing it "right."

That sort of thinking has severely limited with the actor is offering. Because the actor is seeking to do it right, nothing wrong can happen. There will be no surprises or leaps of faith. Comedy cannot be exploited or mined because the actor is tentative in their choices. The performances of these middle 80 actors are polite. And when we act politely, very little happens dramatically.

Getting back to the question about doing anything crazy, the answer is no. If you remember to use your video, you can't do anything crazy. If you remember to use the truth (as we discovered elsewhere in this book) you will have the information you need to help you navigate these choices. To just do anything crazy would be to abandon your video and therefore the characters truth. You would be living entirely in Actor Brain if you make that decision, and our goal is to be (predominantly) in Character Brain.

What we should embrace is a willingness to be one of the 10 worst. That way we can make sure we're using longer arrows. Nice long powerful arrows. The middle 80's arrows are short, our arrows are long. Our arrows get longer when we embrace unreasonableness. It's our willingness to be in the 10 worst that can give us access to being in the 10 best, because our arrows are not tentative or average, they are unreasonable.

Don't be afraid to have long arrows. Even if those arrows are in the wrong directions. In order to get in the top ten, I'm willing to risk being in the bottom ten.

Now what do I find? My longer arrows give me greater freedom. A wider playing field. Instead of the limitations of doing it good, we're playing now in the expansive choices we discover when we are willing to do it wrong. When we take advantage of this, we are - each of us - more uniquely ourselves. The unreasonable choices that you make freely will not be the same choices that other actors are making. What you will discover there is uniquely yours. Now we are not limited by what the line "should" be but the expanded opportunities of the line.

The eighty actors in the middle have not told a bold or profound story. They were caught up in trying to "act good." They made all of the reasonable choices. They hugged the tree trunk.

Taking risks can be very scary. The ten best and worst actors were the leaf dangling at the very end of the branch. Many of us want to scramble back to the trunk where it's safe. But we have to be willing to be the leaf dangling precariously in a high wind. That is the risk we're talking about.

This comes with a big caveat. Don't let the idea of unreasonableness lead you into simply playing aggressive, angry characters. We can (and should) play unreasonably compassionate, unreasonably calm, unreasonably forgiving, unreasonably kind. Being unreasonable doesn't mean loud.

Don't Fix it

Actors often try to fix the language. They seem to think their job is to make the language sound "natural." To take the language and make it flow seamlessly, make it average. Avoid that tendency. Instead of fixing the language, highlight how it is broken.

We can highlight how the language is broken by paying attention to the rhythms of the dialogue. Take advantage of the opportunities the writer has given us through punctuation. The period at the end of the sentence indicates a full stop, the comma indicates a brief pause. If the writer has written a pause into the rhythm, pay attention to it. See what there is to discover by following the writers guidelines.

David Mamet's dialogue is known for its rhythm, its cadence. The language sounds like real speech because of its disregard for syntax, because of the seemingly inconsistent perspectives of the character's speech. These are clues. They are there to be investigated, explored and taken advantage of. Not fixed.

Don't paraphrase. Each line (as written) is an opportunity, not a burden. That line we hate on the first day of rehearsal will probably be our favorite line by closing night. We won't discover what's possible if we aren't willing to investigate.

Improvisation is becoming more and more prevalent in casting decisions. Any serious actor should also study improv. Improv helps us break through the limitations of logic and politeness, giving our characters a wider emotional playing field.

The casting team will let you know if they want you to improvise in your audition. Don't assume you are welcome to change the lines - to improve them or make them sound more "natural." This just indicates a lack of preparation. Give the writer (who is sometimes sitting right there!) their due.

If we are to be the best actors, we will have to complete the magic trick. Take full advantage of what the script offers, while making the writer disappear.

Un-presentability

Actors bravely show what others would hide away. In real life, in people's moments of despair or grief or sensuality, they keep the experience behind closed doors. They hide away their moments of loneliness and sorrow. The average person would not want to be seen this way. We are not average people. We are actors.

It takes courage. In embracing un-presentability we are representing people in their most vulnerable times. By embracing un-presentability, we are sending a message to the audience that the event is a large one. A large event tells a powerful story. The more unpresentable we are, the larger the stakes for our character.

Ruin the Party

There's a great moment in Goodfellas where we see Joe Pesci ruin the party, get belligerent for no apparent reason. The character takes a feel good moment in the scene and reverses it, makes us extremely uncomfortable. That's a great moment. What the actor is doing is embracing the task of ruining the party. It takes a lot of guts to ruin the party. Look at the impoliteness and unreasonableness he is embracing. In fact this may be one of the great ruin the party moments in all of film.

Most actors would not have seen this opportunity so powerfully. Or they may have been tentative because they don't know it's okay to ruin the party. But it's your job to ruin the party. To move your audience out of their comfort zone and leave no room for complacency.

The more powerfully impolite the more memorable. This discomfort is the reason we remember the scene so well that actors talk about it a generation later. It's as impolite as it gets.

Take this principle as far as you can, but stop before you make anyone feel threatened physically, or compromised in any way. Don't make people get worried about safety. Not the casting team and not the other actors. No one will be impressed by how out of control you can get. The casting team will just be worried about their furniture and that you'll sue them if you hurt yourself. Other actors in the scene with you will be speed dialing their agents and union rep. They may be impressed that it looks like you are out of control (if that is what the scene requires) but professionals want to work with professionals.

A lot of actors mistakenly think they have succeeded if they sufficiently "get into it." Your experience is not the one that matters. Don't indulge yourself. The great actors may look out of control, but don't be fooled. They know exactly what they're doing.

Sado/Masochism?

Not to over simplify, but the idea of sadism (inflicting [emotional] pain on yourself while playing your character) and masochism (inflicting [emotional] pain on your character when diagramming your story) are interesting ways for us to approach our character's arcs.

Sadism - when crafting our characters - allows us to raise the stakes on what our characters are experiencing. If it is painful, we will look for ways to increase that pain. We will create more angst, more loss, a larger void in the world of our characters. This raises the tension of our character's predicament and gives our audience a greater need for release, creating a more satisfying dramatic event.

A masochistic approach - when playing our characters - can help in the same way. We can find deeper and more resonant emotional values when we force our characters to confront larger obstacles. There is greater release for our audience when we create greater needs in the roles we play.

In a silent movie, when the hero steps on a banana peel and slips and falls, the pain the character experiences feels good to the audience. They are laughing partly because it didn't happen to them. The Three Stooges style of humor is a testament to this idea. Audiences love pain. We can create a more satisfying experience with this approach. If it doesn't hurt, it doesn't have impact.

CHAPTER 2:
SELF DIRECTION

While performing we can become self-conscious. We can begin to judge our performance and fall into our actor brain. We may have thoughts such as "Say the line like this and it will be funny" or "If I say it like this it will be believable" or "Why aren't they laughing?" or "I'm not doing a very good job. Come on, do better!" All of these thoughts come from actor brain.

Be prepared with the character's Mantra. The mantra is a fundamental thought the character might have repetitively. Do this preparation so that when you decide to dive back into character brain, your mantra will give you a pool to dive into.

A mantra might be "I gotta quit this job." Or "I am in love with you," or "these darn kids," or "I can't handle this right now." These are thoughts that are not included in our dialogue, but the reality of the characters inner world and outlook. To quickly dive back out of actor brain and into character brain, take on the first person thought of your character's mantra.

Literally impose this thought on yourself. Say the line "Will there be anything else?" and use the mantra "I gotta quit this job." You have character brain and actor Brain working together. This does not give your actor brain a chance to judge your work . It is employed in the task of using your mantra and diving back into character brain.

Of course remember that sometimes it is completely appropriate to be in our actor brain. We need actor brain. Actor brain was at rehearsal.

It is when actor brain is not being productive but judging or editing or assessing our work, that we will remember to use mantra. To get away from the disempowerment of actor brain, and into the empowered perspective of character brain.

Remember to have a mantra ready so you know what pool you're driving into whenever actor brain is dominating your experience. Your mantra is a conduit back into character brain.

One, Two, Pineapple

It has long been understood that comedy comes in threes. Let's examine why.

The first beat: Establishes an idea

The second beat: Creates an expectation

The third beat: Surprise

This is the structure of almost any joke. This theory of One, Two, Pineapple shows us why comedy comes in threes. The punchline is (virtually) the opposite of what had been expected. In our example of One, Two, Pineapple. "1" establishes numbers, "2" creates the expectation of three. "Pineapple" is the opposite of three. Of course three doesn't have an opposite so we'll use Pineapple.

To create the expectation of one thing, and then surprise the audience with virtually the opposite of what was expected, creates a large event. The more opposed "Pineapple" is to the expectation (three) the larger the event.

Try this with your friends. Say "I have a joke for you." And then say slowly and deliberately "One. Two. Pineapple." I'll bet they laugh. Or maybe just smile. It's funny to them. The trick is to create the expectation of three.

Of course there isn't anything funny about One, Two, Pineapple. It doesn't need to be funny. It is expectation (1, 2,) and opposing idea (Pineapple) that are the building blocks for humor. And drama.

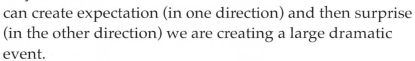

One, two, pineapple is relevant in telling powerful stories. Anytime we can create expectation (in one direction) and then surprise (in the other direction) we are creating a large dramatic event.

Expectation creates tension. If the audience is in a state of expectation - if they cannot wait to see what happens next - you've got them right where you want them. Creating expectation gives the audience the first half of an equation. The second half of that equation will be release (giving the audience what was expected) or quite often surprise (the opposite of what was expected)

Implementing this is simple. Once we see what the punchline (pineapple) is, we can work backwards and try to create an expectation that is as opposed as possible to whatever becomes Pineapple. Or we can see where the story ends and try to create an expectation that is as opposed as possible to what eventually happens.

Call to Action

To tell a powerful story we have to affect the audience so they're different people after the show than when they came in. To be a different person when they stand up, from the one that sat down. They're changed because they've been inspired and moved by the experience.

It doesn't always have to be profound, but in each scene or role or story we can look for the opportunity to change the world. It can be anything from "let's not make war on each other" to "let's keep a tidier desk." This call to action could be in something as basic as do the right thing, be a better person, have compassion. When our characters are awakened can we awaken our audience as well?

We can identify the Call to Action by recognizing how we want our audience to change. Do we want them to behave differently? Have a new awareness? Do we want to powerfully expose societal evils such as homophobia, racism and misogyny? Each time we have an audience, we have the opportunity, and even the responsibility, to evoke change.

Your favorite cop show may inspire you to be a bit more heroic. Your favorite musical may inspire you to be more confident or fight harder for justice. Society will behave like the people they admire so in a larger sense our job is to be admired, to be worthy of that admiration. And to consider what behavior we are hoping to inspire, how exactly we are hoping to change the world.

Of course, not all of the examples we're going to provide will be positive. Just as often we can enact positive change through the negative example. We can move an audience to change by powerfully representing what needs to be changed. We can tell the loving story by showing the absence of love, by demonstrating a vacuum that only love can fill.

There is also a great opportunity when playing roles of people we do not admire. To even play people we would hate. There is tremendous power in indicting the audience. To shine a light on what needs to be exposed and show each of us how ugly our behavior can be. After all, it is quite possible (and maybe even likely) that somewhere in the audience tonight is someone who is abusive or someone who behaves cruelly or takes advantage of others. Can we seize the opportunity to show how ugly that behavior is?

We can see powerful examples in The Laramie Project and God's Country. These plays shine their light on the ugliness of bigotry. To do that in a polite manner would be a disservice. Without confronting it head on, the audience will not see the need for change.

It follows that when we take responsibility to change the world we now have to consider "toward what?" The call to action is (in almost every instance) for the audience to tune into the love in their lives — to appreciate the love that they have more, to try to repair or grieve where love has been lost or be inspired to love again.

All great art is about love or protest. (Protest is actually about the absence of love) Looking for the opportunity of the love in our work, or the denial of love in our characters, can cause the audience to leave changed, enlightened and empowered by our performance. This love is not only about people. It may be the love of justice or playing the trombone.

It may be the love of compassion or money. But it's always about love. That's the only thing anyone cares about.

Our audience is made up of individuals. Each person entering our performance with their own history and point of view. If we are to engage each of these individuals in our work, we will want to challenge them, confront them.

Put the audience in the most difficult position possible. Provide no easy answers. When our characters are faced with choices, make them as difficult as possible. For each yes, balance it with a no. For every positive, have a negative. How difficult can we make our choice? The more difficult we make the predicament, the more invested our audience will be in the choice our character will make.

This is often referred to as "Raising the Stakes." Making the events in our character's lives into *important* events in our character's lives. When our character makes a decision, the event becomes larger if it is more difficult to make, more impactful when there are greater consequences.

If the answers are easy, we are letting the audience (and ourselves) off the hook. We are giving them (and ourselves) the easy way out. Instead put the audience (and yourself) in the most difficult position possible, and then tighten the screws a bit more. We want to create a powerful experience.

Many people suggest that the greatest line ever written in English is from Shakespeare in Hamlet's line "To be or not to be." In fact, it is the one line of dialogue that has come to mean drama itself. Out of every line ever written by anybody, let alone Shakespeare, why this line? Why has it come to be the one that means drama? Let's break it down.

71

It is a comparison of the two most opposing ideas in the most succinct construct. Note that the comparison of opposing ideas are not Philadelphia/Pittsburgh or red/blue. These two opposing ideas (being/not being) encompass all other ideas, that's how opposing they are. They encompass every other emotional possibility.

We can find opportunities to create the same type of dynamism in our work. To compare a character's future to the past, to compare what will happen if you do or don't take the next step, to compare how you felt before or after an event – any of these comparisons tell the core story more powerfully. Comparisons give the audience a very digestible dramatic equation.

Let's look at the comparison between before/after. If before an event your character has one characteristic, but after the event a change in that characteristic, the event is given significance. The greater the change, the greater the event. By demonstrating a profound change, we tell the story of a profound event.

Let's look at the comparison of either/or. The more profoundly different the outcomes of the either/or scenario, the more important the decision your character might make. If the either/or outcome is similar, then the equation itself isn't a powerful one. The audience is less invested in the choice your character makes. To highlight the difference between those outcomes, helps the audience care more about which decision you're going to make.

It's easy to see the opportunity for comparison in either/or and before/after. But there are many more ways to find opportunities for comparisons in our text. Words like "sometimes, maybe, I hope, if" – there's a million of them – "perhaps, I think" – the list goes on – all of these are opportunities to heighten the comparative idea - giving weight to whatever it is you're discussing.

Sometimes there is comparison in our dialogue but there are also comparisons in our juxtaposition of ideas. If - when our character describes an event - the audience can grasp the consequences of it happening versus not happening, that is twice the information than that it simply happened. It gives the event significance.

We want the audience to see both sides of our coin. We're potentially doubling the amount of information they get. Not only what is happening but what isn't, not only what we want but what we don't want.

Taken a step further - and this is significant - everything we say is more powerful when it is compared to everything we don't say. A chair is more powerful when compared to a table, than it is by itself. When we highlight the comparisons in our dialogue, our language carves a bolder path.

Emphasis

The word we stress will automatically provide a comparison. Let's look at a sample line of simple dialogue:

"I went to the bank."
Where we place the stress will communicate the comparison.

For instance:

"**I** went to the bank." implies a comparison to "**You** went to the bank."

"I **went** to the bank." implies a comparison to "I **came from** the bank."

"I went **to** the bank." implies a comparison to "I went **away from** the bank."

"I went to **the** bank." implies a comparison to "I went to **a** bank."

"I went to the **bank**." implies a comparison to "I went to the **store**."

In each of these cases, we can communicate two sides to the statement. The one that is, as well as the one that isn't. With this, we can highlight why our dialogue matters. What we say also presents what we don't say. The audience gets twice the information. And a more impactful experience.

The audience doesn't attend or tune in to see *a moment* in our character's lives, they attend or tune in to see *the moment* in our character's lives.

Look for the opportunity to play the scene as a Life Moment for your character. The opportunity is there for this moment to be a life-changing one. From this moment on - in ways small and large - our characters will never be the same. Show us that moment. It is available in almost every scene.

Is there a way to tell the story that "this has never happened before?" That "this is the one time my character would respond in this particular way?" If our characters are driven past their reason, this powerfully tells the story that this moment is unprecedented. Therefore it is important for our audience to be there.

Also consider it this way: there is life before the event, and there is life after the event. The more contrast between before and after, the greater the event. Audiences want to be privy to great events. They will tune in again next week to see life-changing moments. Turning points in our characters lives indicate large dramatic events. If the moment is not life-changing, then the audience doesn't need to watch. There is very little to see.

We can be sure to fight hard on behalf of our characters by avoiding a few words commonly used by actors. In rehearsals, I always have an alarm bell in my ear when I hear an actor say that the character is "just" this. Or "only" that or "kind of" something or "a little" of something else.

Let's stop using limiting words from our dramatic inquiry such as "just" "a little" "kind of" or "only." It is not dramatically interesting for our character to be "a little" invested in something. We diminish our opportunities when we make such limited investments in our characters.

The audience will feel a sense of intimacy with you if they know something about your character that the other character you're in the scene with doesn't. If they are in on your secret, you make them your confidante.

If the audience knows something that the other character does not, they feel closer to you than the person in the scene with you. We can provide for them, an Intimate Glimpse.

This is a very common construct in scene work. Your character may be telling the boss you were at the doctor's office this afternoon but the audience knows (or suspects) it isn't true. Or you say that you are happy about your promotion but the audience thinks you may be scared. By letting the audience have a pact with you, you can deepen your bond with them.

Pretend So Hard that you are no longer in a casting office or theatre, you are now in another land or time. Pretend So Hard at the audition that even the people you are auditioning for believe your reality, not theirs.

We can sometimes be disempowered by playing ideas like vulnerability, sensuality, grief, fear, etc. Pretend So Hard can overcome the disbelief that is naturally going to be there. It helps us overcome that self-consciousness we may feel in playing those emotions.

Children can naturally Pretend So Hard. We want to invite this type of playful, adventurous and free creativity. This can help us overcome our own perceived limitations, our own disconnect with the material, and help us uncover the emotional values required on behalf of the character.

In the cold audition room or green screen setting or in the artifice of a studio set, Pretend So Hard can help us overcome the inherent dis-realities of a working environment. On the TV or movie set when you look off into the distance (and the camera captures a beautiful shot of you) what you're actually seeing is the crew and the lighting equipment and the craft services table. When we Pretend So Hard, your character can see the sunset over your farm and your vision for the future.

We can use it to help transport ourselves and our audience. Potentially when you Pretend So Hard, even those in the cast and crew (who are part of this dis-reality) can be taken with you to where you say the scene takes place. We have to overcome all doubt. Including our own.

Some actors may take the approach of "Well when it's real, that's when I'll fully invest. Once I have all the props, know all my blocking, once I have everything memorized, then I'll fully invest." With that mindset, we're not going to become great magicians anytime soon.

This approach helps us make that leap from wherever we are to performance level by diving deeper into our character's waters. We all know what it's like to pretend. As children, we did it easily. You have an obligation to the scene, the moment, the character, the director and the writer. And to yourself. An obligation to Pretend So Hard.

The Magic Trick only works when it has staying power. The magic has to last after the trick is finished. Otherwise the audience will discover it wasn't magic at all. This would rob them of the experience. That powerful moment would lose all of its impact. To combat this, Plant Your Flag.

In the "moment after the moment," don't bail out on your choice or performance. It is in this "moment after the moment" that you finish the Magic Trick. If we don't plant our flag, the audience will see that what they thought was magic wasn't really magic at all.

When on camera don't bail out on your scene after the last line. Stay in the scene until you hear the T of the word "Cut." There is an element of Aggressive Act here. "I am not going to be pushed off my mountain. I have taken this territory and I will defend it." If no one says "cut," be willing to stay in character through the weekend.

Planting our flag helps us be emotionally economical as well. It helps us tell a clean story instead of one that is cluttered. The economical emotional story will be most powerful.

Actors may often play three emotional values in a moment when one emotional value would have been stronger. One reason we do this is because we are uncertain about our choices. When we are uncertain about our choices we tend to leap frog from one choice to another without ever planting our flag in the one that is most powerful.

It takes a lot of guts to plant your flag. You have to be willing to stare doubt in the eye and overcome it. That doubt might come from the camera lens, the audience, casting director or your scene partner. Our tendency may be to become timid if we feel challenged. Let's plant our flag and stand ready to defend.

Fighting Hard for Our Characters

If we get the opportunity to play any role, we have a responsibility to fight hard. Our characters cannot speak for themselves. We must speak boldly on their behalf. That is what actors do. Let's afford all of our characters equal investment. Whether they're historical characters or fictional ones, leading roles or walk-ons.

The Magic Trick is that we're not actors at all but that we are the characters. Wouldn't it go a long way towards being a good magician if we could fight harder for our characters than we are fighting for ourselves? Let's not fight for the actor in the room, let's fight for the character.

Fighting harder for our characters than we are fighting for ourselves helps us to quiet any Actor Brain counter-productivity such as "I hope I get this job" or "I hope I'm acting good." (To seek the audience's approval is, in itself, a position of weakness) Fighting hard for our characters helps us stop fighting for ourselves and creates the Magic Trick.

For example, in a scene where your character is on a job interview, you have the opportunity to represent the universal idea of needing a job. To fight hard for your character is to represent all those who have ever needed a job. They are not in the room right now to fight for themselves. You are. Fight hard.

When we explore the most compelling dramatic possibilities for the character that needs a job, we may create a scenario that includes taking care of a sick relative, lots of debt, an empty refrigerator, or creditors at the door. The Universal Idea of needing a job may consist of the most desperate circumstances.

Is it in the audience's best interest that you fight hard for your character? Is it in the audience's best interest for your characters to care deeply about their own lives and those around them? Obviously the answer is yes.

Never underestimate the needs or the plight of people. Somewhere there is someone who really needs our help. They don't have the platform that we have. We can give them a voice. We have the opportunity and the responsibility to fight hard for them. They are all around us. Sometimes it is even us.

Actors are here to change the world. Culturally, actors point the way to a better tomorrow for all of us. We should always be in touch with our opportunity to evoke change in the community, and in the world at large. We have to take advantage of the platform we're being given to lead the way. Let's fight hard. Can you fight hard for someone you don't know? You are an actor. Of course you can.

Square Mile of Ocean

In a square mile of ocean, if you could measure every current and temperature and living organism - you could measure it forever and it would never be the same twice. Human beings are a square mile of ocean. It would be plastic or false to try to pretend otherwise.

The currents and temperatures of our human experience cannot be predicted or controlled or dictated. When we embrace this concept in our work, it begins to feel okay to not know. It feels natural to respond to the give and take of our character's moments. Instead of trying to control our performance, we are giving ourselves over to a State of Not Knowing.

The blood in our veins is a Square Mile of Ocean. It is not 100% predictable or repeatable. Our blood cells will continuously flow, we cannot predict or control where a cell will be in any given moment. Because we are constantly in a new state, we don't want to predict the tides or the nuances of our selves in performance, instead we'll embrace the uncertainty of a Square Mile of Ocean.

Style

All of our work has style to it. We don't want to discover it after we have already auditioned. We can (and should) be proactive in our application of style. The actor who gets the job (all things being equal) will be the one who best understands and embraces style.

Let's identify a few styles. This is by no means a definitive list, nor should we consider them to be answers (remember answers are dead ends) We won't use style as a limitation, but as a possibility.

Realism - Gritty, unflinching, adult subject matter
Farce - Fast, funny, pie in the face humor
Romantic Comedy - Misunderstandings, love, relationships
Musical Theatre - Singing, broad acting
Mystery - Chilling, suspenseful
Horror - Scary, often violent
Science Fiction - Futuristic, space aliens, invasion
Western - Macho, good guys vs bad guys
Action - Same as above

Historical - Period piece, often biographical

Teen Comedy - Rude humor, kids vs parents / teachers, bullies and nerds

Family Drama - Parents and children, coming of age, life lessons

Children's Entertainment - Teaching, simple storytelling, songs

Soap Opera - Melodrama, marital affairs, power struggles

The same line of dialogue in Horror style will be markedly different from the delivery in Children's Entertainment style. Teen Comedy is quite different from Science Fiction, etc.

Every script will be unique in style. Once we begin to understand and embrace style, we see the possibilities will vary with each. Our inquiry before the audition and during rehearsals is how to embrace the style that presents the material in its best light.

How do we embrace style? Think of it as a shifting of your center - a style shift. If we are suddenly cast in the role of a soldier, we have to be living in a different world where different rules apply. The same if we are cast as a farmer or doctor. To be someone else, we have to shake off who we really are. To shift our center is to carry ourselves differently, assertively change our point of view.

In a melodramatic style, we may find ourselves placing our wrist to the forehead, or twirling our mustache. In teen comedy style, perhaps we play with higher energy and naiveté. Our job with the script is to make it it's best - whatever that might be. To understand and embrace the style of *this* material. This gives us opportunities to boldly change the rules on everyday life, and provide our audience with a new reality.

A lot of actors may feel disempowered by style. That acting in a performance for children automatically means we will lose integrity in our work. Or that because we are in a musical, we can't expect the same standards of ourselves as in a straight play. Just as some actors think drama is "more important" than comedy.

We may be in a "silly" comedy or melodrama, but we can't know how badly some members of our audience may need to laugh at something silly or yell "boo" at a bad guy. It can be a tremendous relief and often desperately needed. We shouldn't underestimate the potential of our performance or judge the material (or our audiences) negatively.

Style is fluid. Do not think in terms of one-size-fits-all. In fact the style of one line may vary from the style of the next. We don't apply style to limit us. We use it to find opportunities and inspire our choices.

Exercise: Style

Refer to the list of styles earlier in this chapter. Add a couple of others (Opera, Pantomime) for fun. Choose a few lines of dialogue from scripts you have. Perform your dialogue while embracing each of these styles.

Doing this exercise will uncover interesting "readings" of your dialogue. You may even discover "That thing I thought couldn't possibly work, *can* work." It will provide a more expansive list of possibilities for the character and the moment.

Odd Couple Diagram

In Neil Simon's The Odd Couple, the two main characters (Oscar and Felix) are diametrically opposed. Two friends - the sloppiest character imaginable and the neatest character imaginable - become roommates. Each takes their point of view to unreasonable extremes. It is the contrast between the two characters that gives the relationship its dynamics.

We can use this equation to our advantage by highlighting the differences between the characters. When Sherlock Holmes-ing, do you see one character is assertive? That can be a clue that the other is timid. Is one character powerful? The other is probably powerless.

If we discover that both characters are powerful, we can look for this opposition elsewhere. Perhaps one is honest and the other isn't. Highlight this aspect then. If they're both dishonest maybe one is experienced and the other isn't. This opposition is there somewhere. Find it and make it part of your story.

When the audience clearly understands one character's perspective (sloppiness drives Felix crazy) they know what to expect when Oscar makes a mess. This anticipation of Felix' response is active and vibrant for the audience.

The audience can't care about you, if they know nothing about you. Paint with bold colors. When the audience knows something about you, they can begin to have an expectation. On the following page, the events on the right are more powerful because of the character trait on the left.

What the audience knows:	What happens:
You're kind	You meet someone in need
You're greedy	You find a bag of money
You're jealous	The phone rings and hangs up
You're shy	You have to give a speech

This type of diagram doesn't have to be so on-the-nose. For instance:

What the audience knows:	What Happens:
You're kind	The phone rings and hangs up
You're greedy	You meet someone in need
You're jealous	You have to give a speech
You're shy	You find a bag of money

The juxtaposition of these ideas can enhance our story and make it more powerful, even profound. The character description may not define this. You have to investigate and find the juxtaposition that will best serve the audience's experience.

Gilligan Diagram

In the television show House, we see a doctor with a terrible bedside manner. In Gilligan's Island, we see a first mate who trips over his own shoelaces. The audience enjoys the experience of seeing our characters overcome our natural obstacles.

In the teen movie where the boy has a crush on the popular girl, usually the boy is very unpopular at first. The power of the story is in him overcoming tremendous obstacles. If our characters are ill-equipped at the job they are handed, we create a large obstacle for them to overcome.

In My Fair Lady we see this as our story. If Eliza in act one is middle-class, her journey to upper-class is not a large event. By being a girl from the gritty and grimy lower-class streets of London, her transformation to Lady becomes a large event.

Let's take this example and apply it to our work. If our character hopes to woo a girl, let's be sure to present a large obstacle; shyness, tongue-tied, awkward, clumsy etc. If our character is running for office, let's make him ill-equipped for the job by being dishonest or having a quick temper. This opportunity is quite often not found on the page. That is, it is not in your dialog. It is not necessarily in your character arc or even your story as written.

Continuity

On the film set the idea of continuity can be very disempowering for actors because you spend your second take worrying a lot about what you did in your first take. Or the reverse which is spending a lot of energy in your first take trying to remember in detail what you'll do for your second take.

One thing we should consider is this: the editor is not going to use both ways you said the line. They're going to pick one. So that take we think we're supposed to match doesn't exist.

Your second take isn't different because you want it to be different. It's different because our characters didn't do take one. The actor did that. So the character is living it for the first time regardless of which take it is. From that perspective it's not important that your take is different, only that it is existing in a state of surprise.

Once again keep an Ace of Clubs on this. It isn't necessary anyone sees you outwardly making different choices, what is most important is that we put the idea of continuity into its proper perspective.

Our responsibility then, is to allow change in what we're doing in the second take and not do the same thing. So the editor has a choice between the two. Giving them options. We don't need two copies of the same DVD. We want a different take.

If you ever happen to be in the fortunate situation where you are offered a take at the end of shooting a scene, be sure to say yes. Directors might call this the "one for nothing" take. In this opportunity they are confident they have the footage they need to fundamentally tell the story. This is your opportunity to break the rules of the scene. Contradict the character. Embrace again what does not make sense.

Where the sameness does come in, take to take, is in matching physically. You were holding a drink? You've got to be holding a drink in take two. The physical aspects of when you set the glass down, where you put it, when you pick up the gun, how you hold it, those things do have to match, take to take. The physicality (the outer life) has to match, but not the inner life of the character.

CHAPTER 3:
VOICE AND BODY

Proactive Musicality

Musicality is present in all of our speech. Musical values such as tone, pitch, intervals, intonation, rhythm, syncopation, leading tone, and resolve are present in all of our speech all of the time. This understanding presents an interesting question: "Which musicality?"

It may be easily understood that a minor key creates a different emotional dynamic than a major key. In films, the music is usually in a minor key during tense or scary scenes and in a major key for the happy scenes. Is it possible for us to understand and employ such musical tactics to inform and move our audiences? Yes.

We often use the phrase to illustrate this "It was a dark and stormy night." If this is our line of dialogue, we can see the opportunity of musicality. Imagine saying this line

around a campfire as a ghost story. What musicality might you use for this line?

When you infuse musicality into this line of dialogue, you are providing for the audience not only the information contained within the line, but you are also communicating context and tone.

Productive Pause

Here is a drawing of a pause. We go. We stop going. We go again.

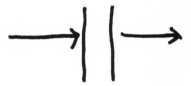

During a pause, there are two productive experiences possible for our audience. In one pause, the audience's active experience is to *reflect* on what has just been said.

In another pause, the audience's active experience is to *anticipate* what will be said next.

In each pause, the audience is experiencing something. Either reflecting or anticipating.

Usually, the more powerful of these is the pause in which the audience reflects upon what you have said. In this moment the audience may be nodding their heads in agreement with you. They're thinking things like "That is so true" or "I agree with you." In fact, the power of the line, is greatly enhanced in the pause that comes after.

In this case, which we will call the reflective pause, the power of our words is enhanced. The statement our character has made has left a lasting impression in the audience's mind. This adds power to *what was said*.

In the second type of pause, the audience is anticipating what is to come. Consider a line like, "I know who the murderer was. It was (pause) the butler."

The pause placed before the resolution of the line builds the audience's tension toward that resolution. During this, which we will call the anticipatory pause, tension is built as the audience anticipates *what you are going to say*.

Theoretically the longer the pause the greater the power of what follows it. But be careful. Tension demands release. If it isn't released by you smartly you will lose the opportunity. So a big Ace of Clubs on this technique. Tension is a balloon easily burst without release.

So now that we have identified the two types of pauses that we will find active for our audience, how do we help dictate which experience they are to have? If we have identified which type of a pause we are hoping for the moment, how do we then employ that knowledge? How do we evoke in our audience the experience we are hoping for them to have?

To address this, let's look at leading tones.

Leading Tones

In the diatonic scale, leading tones are in the number two and seven position. In the key of C, the leading tones are the number two (D) and number seven (B)

In the key of C, when we play a B natural or D, we cannot resolve on those notes. They are called leading tones because they lead you to the tone one or eight. The tension created does not allow resolution while on the leading tone. We can create tension simply through our choice of pitch. This is extremely useful to us in communicating powerfully with our audience. This leading tone pitch can create tension so that our audience' cheeks may feel flushed or they may get goosebumps. Through choice of pitch, we can cause a visceral reaction in our audience. In this application we are not even dependent upon content. Merely upon application of leading tone.

Putting it simply, to create a reflective pause we will use a resolved tone, and to create a pause of anticipation, we use a leading tone.

Syncopation

Syncopation is "away" from the rhythm. The concept is to establish a rhythm and then upset it, establish a rhythm and then upset it.

You might think of it as speaking between the beats. The text as it *coincides* with the rhythm, does not cut through to the audience's ear, as much as the text in *juxtaposition* to the rhythm.

What we call "comic timing" is very much an application of this idea. The syncopated beat is also unexpected. The syncopated beat cuts through to the ear of the audience, and takes them by surprise. This contributes to the comedic event.

Surprise is a necessary component of comedy. To accentuate the offbeat, will take your audience by surprise - when it is contrasted with the established beat.

When we are applying the idea of rhythm here, it is not merely the rhythm of the language, it is the rhythm of the moment, the scene. The rhythm is fluid and ever-changing and so is how we apply syncopation. It is not necessarily the same from night to night, performance to performance. The rhythm is a living, breathing thing.

Falling in Love With Consonants.

Take advantage of the opportunities consonants create. This will energize our communication. There are five opportunities in a word like "strict." If an actor has the opportunity to say that beautiful word, take advantage of all the visceral experience of a beautiful sound like "ct." How about a word like "burst?" Energizing the consonants can keep the audience's ear awake. It also adds conviction to our language. Not only for the audience, but for us too.

Of course it also has the added bonus of helping to assure that everything you say is understood. There are very few cardinal sins in acting, but a major one is if your audience asks, "What did he say?" Taking advantage of consonants helps assure this will not be their experience. Any time the audience is not sure they heard you correctly, they'll be pulled out of the story.

Consonants are opportunities.

Aunt Enid

Especially stress consonants when we say words that will surprise the audience's ear. Adding energy to the surprise word helps prevent them from doubting what it was you said. This allows them to digest the information assured in the knowledge they did not mis-hear it. We certainly can't communicate powerfully if our words are not understood.

Maybe you have a line like: "After work we're all going over to Aunt Enid's house. You want to go?"

But the audience hears "After work we're all going over to a Neenid's house. You want to go?" This leaves our audience wondering: "What's a Neenid?"

These words or phrases come up consistently. Often they are names of characters, or proper nouns in general such as cities and towns. But it is not limited to those phrases. Use extra energy and articulation anytime the audience's ear will be surprised.

When you have an Aunt Enid moment in the script, be sure to give emphasis to your pronunciation. Your instincts may tell you to also pause briefly before and perhaps even after you say the Aunt Enid. Just make sure that you raise your need to communicate. If you raise your need to communicate high enough, Aunt Enid will take care of herself.

Tip: Concentrate on both Verbal Energy (articulation, movements of the tongue, pitch, open vowels) and Vocal Energy (projection, diaphragmatic support, breathing, relaxed throat)

The Need to Communicate

In moments where things are feeling flat, raising the need to communicate can make your stakes bigger. Raising the Need to Communicate also covers a number of other actor problems including diction and projection.

Picture a scene where you are seeing a small child in potential danger. "GET. AWAY. FROM. THAT. RIGHT. NOW!"

The urgency of the situation causes your diction to improve. Your projection too. The need to communicate has taken care of both of these ideas. So can we take this concept and apply it elsewhere in our text?

Another benefit is that raising the need to communicate in the dialogue, raises the urgency and momentum of the scene.

This approach is helpful when the director says "be louder," or "speak more clearly." For you to execute the note of being louder or speaking more clearly, you would have to be in your Actor Brain. Raising the Need to Communicate solves this problem in Character Brain.

Embodiment of Emotions

Where do emotions come from? Within. Each of us has the potential for any emotion on the spectrum. Somewhere inside each of us is each emotion, even those that we try to never use. Anger, greed, cruelty... they're all in there somewhere.

There are physical symptoms of our emotional states. When we are feeling genuine emotions, they may manifest in physical sensations such as an upset stomach, butterflies, racing pulse or a heavy heart. If we try to get in touch with the physical embodiment of an emotional value, we can find that emotion.

When we are nervous for instance, our hands may tremble and our voice may quiver. If we tremble our hand and quiver our voice, can we create nervousness? When we feel proud, our posture improves and our eye-line rises. If we stand taller and raise our eyes, can we embody pride? Yes.

Initially, it may feel "fake" to try these tactics. That's okay. We need to generate these emotional values. Then we can truthfully live in their waters, understand their currents. We will need to generate them from somewhere.

Each of us will feel emotional values in different ways.

Exercise: Emotional Embodiment

In a quiet environment, clear your mind. Choose an emotion. (Some are listed below for reference) Physically locate and identify where that emotion lies within yourself. Focus your intentions in this area of your body. Take advantage of what you discover.

Suggested emotions:
Loneliness
Pride
Compassion
Nervousness
Ambition

Group Exercise: "People who are..."

Take suggestions from the class to make a list of characteristics by completing the phrase "People who are..." For example lazy, sloppy, excited, morose, ignorant, caring, generous, etc. Write them on the board, coming up with about 20 different characteristics.

Each student should choose five at random and write them down. Then give each student a couple lines of dialogue from scripts you have. (It's best if these scripts are not too stylized) Give each student a couple of minutes to look at their text. Then have the actors say their lines one by one in the manner of each characteristic they wrote down. Say the lines the way a "lazy" person would, then an "ignorant" person and so forth. The other actors can try to guess each characteristic.

Tell students not to worry about "winning" this game. Use it to explore emotional values in your body. It also helps us discover the possibilities of the line without restricting ourselves to the logical line reading.

Economy of Motion

Dance and choreography are good examples when it comes to economy of motion. The choreographer trims our physicality to the essential and gives us all the motions the piece requires. We cannot also do other motions. When acting - and all of our movements aren't choreographed - our instincts should embrace the same economy of motion.

If the choreographer has asked us to move our right hand, we do not also move our left. If the choreographer has asked us for a particular head turn, we do not also move our arms. Economy is the power in this equation. Without economy all power is lost.

The choreographer might require a sudden, crisp extension of the forearm and hand. It is on one very specific count of the music. The movement is sudden. It is brisk. It is purposeful. And the story that the bodies are telling is powerful because of it.

Consider a photograph. Economy of Motion gives the audience a clear image. Without economy, the image is blurry. The strong actor (with the help of a good director) simply creates a series of strong, powerful images. To think of one as flowing into the other is a disservice. Think in terms of a series of sharp and focused images.

For purposes of powerful performance, we should take away anything that is not necessary and not serving our purpose. Any physical motion that is not assisting in the storytelling, is detracting from it.

When we use economy of motion we are not distracting the audience's eye. And when we give the audience a clear and in focus picture, they will zoom in - even from the back row - to what they really want to see: our eyes.

Let the Audience In

The eyes are the windows to the inside, the avenues to intimacy. In fact, they are the only place on our bodies that are not covered with skin. When we reunite with an old friend, we focus on their eyes. When we fall in love, the eyes are what we fall into. Because we care about people, we look there for emotional clues. To help the audience care about our characters, we will have to give them access to our eyes so they can look for emotional clues in us.

We don't look directly at the audience or camera in most cases. Usually, we pretend they aren't there at all, so we will divert our eye-line to be just above the audience's eye-line. On stage our neutral eye-line should be slightly above the back row. On camera, slightly above the camera lens and a bit to one side.

By keeping our eye-line slightly higher than the audience's, we are allowing them "in," giving them access. No one can fall in love with you through your eyelids. We have to be able to see "in" to feel intimacy with your character.

The theatre audience who is below your eye-line will feel included because they can see in, they have access. The audience that is above your eye-line will be seeing your brow, your eyelids. This won't give them access to care about you. Raise your eye-line so everyone can get an intimate look.

When auditioning, it is best to not make eye contact with the casting team. If you make eye contact, you are controlling where they look. When you do this, you are not giving them the anonymity to look wherever they choose.

If you have to create an imaginary scene partner - someone you can address your monologue to - place your imaginary scene partner downstage (toward the audience) instead of to your left or right. They're imaginary, so we might as well place them where we are giving the audience or casting team access to our eyes. Placing our imaginary scene partner downstage does this.

Whenever possible, on camera use your real scene partner to establish your eye-line. Don't worry too much about staying open to the camera. A good cinematographer and director will place the camera and block the scene to help you keep your eyes available. Your job is to ignore the camera.

On the stage or set the lights can be very bright and may feel overpowering, causing us to want to shield our eyes from the glare.

Lights are your friend. In class we use the phrase: "Beyonce' that light." Beyonce, the famous singer, would not hide from the spotlight. She basks in its warmth. We need to take on the lights as if they are sunshine on a cold day. The light feeds us.

Don't cause your eyes any damage of course. Never stare directly at the lights but make use of them to be seen. If the light is hurting your eyes a bit, try to get used to it. Frankly, if your eyes hurt a bit, you're well lit.

A good on camera technique in a brightly lit scene is to follow these steps. When they are just about to start filming (someone will say something like "Quiet on the set!") lightly close your eyes.

Look (with eyes closed!) toward the brightest light. About 5 seconds is enough. Just before "Action" turn away from the bright light, into the scene and then open your eyes. Your eyes will be more comfortable because you have gently gotten them used to a bright environment.

Finding Out

In many acting classes, a lot of emphasis is placed on listening to the other actor. Listening however, is not really the right word. Whenever actors start concentrating on listening, they start "ear acting," (cocking their head toward the other actor, sticking their ears out) as if listening were done with the ears. No. Hearing is what is done with the ears.

Instead of the idea of listening, "Find out." Finding Out is listening, but with our heart, our gut. We find out, not only with our ears, but also with our other senses. We find out by intently watching, by observing what the other actor is doing physically; the facial expressions, the body language, the gestures and the nuances of the eyes. We are sensing

their energy. Our ears are only a part of the listening equation.

When we actively "find out" during our work, we can be surprised by what we discover. We are surprised not only by what the other person is saying, but also how they feel about what they are saying and even more importantly, how *we* feel about what they're saying. It adds weight and consequence to the other person's lines. Finding out helps keep us in a state of surprise, because we are learning as we live, finding out as we go, looking for clues, like in real life.

Many actors have trouble when waiting to speak. They are fine while talking but uncomfortable between their lines. Raising our need to find out reminds us that our characters are always moving forward emotionally. They don't only move forward when talking, but also when not talking. By finding out, we can remain fluid in our character's world, instead of the stop-start world of you talk - I talk.

When working on camera, a lot of actors have a tendency to blink excessively. Blinking is a way of hiding from your audience. We can overcome this habit through raising our need to find out. Picture yourself asking your lover "Will you marry me?" In the moment while waiting for the answer, our need to find out will not let us blink. If we blink we may miss a crucial piece of information in our lover's facial expression or the subtlest flicker in the eyes.

Raising our need to find out helps us take a note from actor brain (don't blink so much) and turn it into a character brain behavior. It also gives weight to the other character's lines and story.

Take Up Space

The most charismatic actors can "fill the stage" or "fill the screen." Part of what they are doing is taking up space. Becoming their largest selves. So large that it doesn't stop at the physical self, they can "fill the room" with their presence.

Actors sometimes close themselves off by collapsing at the waist and leaning forward. They seem to be "leading with" the chin, nose or forehead. If we avoid this closed down posture we can ultimately feel more comfortable and empowered.

In elementary school, your gym teacher might have said "Stick out your chest!" He was trying to help with your posture. What we actually want to "lead with" is the clavicle. When we present with the clavicle it puts us in alignment. We become our full height. Best of all, we feel more powerful and communicate more powerfully.

Of course sometimes, you may play characters that are closed off. Perhaps you are playing someone without confidence. The character may be closed off but you - as "the athlete" - are not. Make your everyday posture a confident and powerful one, then change it if the role requires. Remember that *you* need confidence even if your character doesn't have any. We have to powerfully portray those without power.

You Can (Probably) Sing

Many of us mistakenly think that we can't sing. Often when we were kids, we were told by our older brother or

Dad that our singing was terrible. Maybe they covered their ears to demonstrate how bad it was. And many of us live our lives thinking they were right - that we can't sing.

There *are* people who cannot sing, who will never be able to sing. People who are tone-deaf will never be able to sing on pitch, no matter how hard they try.

Only about 5% of the population is tone-deaf. That one person in twenty will never learn to be a good singer. If you happen to be in this special group, you should feel free to raise your voice as loud as you want. But odds are - Reader - you are not one of them.

For the rest of us - the 95% - singing (and doing it in tune) is possible. We can improve as singers, regardless of where we begin. It's just a question of whether we make the effort. If we do, we can vastly improve our chances of forging a career. (Musicals have large casts!) If we're willing to put in the effort, we will improve. It's that simple. Never mind what our older brother said.

CHAPTER 4:
IT'S YOUR TURN

The Relationship That Matters Most

The single most dominant relationship we will nurture is the one between "ourselves" and "ourselves in the role of actor." That's the relationship that is most complex and matters most. And that's the relationship that is most fragile.

It is here where we most often stumble. This is where nerves and doubt live. Preparation and technique are within this relationship as well. This is also where "truth" exists. We need truth in order to be good actors.

The possibilities we see for the character are directly related to our ability to see possibility in the first place. How we are feeling about ourselves directly relates to the quality of what we can offer. The relationship between "me and myself as actor" is the relationship we need to develop because that's the one that is performing. That's the relationship that matters in real time in front of your audience or camera.

How we respond to direction, or at an audition, will be in this relationship as well. That our confidence isn't shaken and our mind is open to make the adjustments. Technique, experience, instincts... they're all in this relationship.

At our most powerful, we are equal measures heightened concentration and heightened relaxation. Extremely high concentration and equally high relaxation. One cannot dominate the other. For each of us the balance might be different. We naturally have more concentration so we need to bring relaxation as an adjustment or vice versa. Either way, we want to be both heightened and balanced.

If we have heightened concentration without relaxation, we are in our heads and cannot live in the moment. If we have heightened relaxation with less concentration, then we

107

might find ourselves undisciplined and give a blasé performance. Finding a balance between relaxation and concentration, both in a heightened state, helps us excel in high stakes moments. The execution of the task to its utmost (concentration) paired in equal measure with confidence and flow (relaxation)

If we can find that alignment we will create from a powerful perspective, which helps us fight harder for our characters. From that ideal perspective, our work can flow.

Actor Cake

Confidence is to the actor, what flour is to the cake. A cake has icing, sprinkles, food coloring and spices, but the single largest ingredient is flour. In our actor cake the single largest ingredient is confidence.

Don't be confident because, darn it, you're pretty. Don't be confident because you deserve it. Don't be confident because each of us has a basic right to feel good about ourselves. Don't be confident because you are very talented. Or any of the other million things we've told ourselves in the past. Be confident because that is your job.

At an audition, on opening night or when the cameras are rolling, rising to the occasion is what is required of us.

108

That's why they chose us, to point the lights at. Because that's expected.

One of the biggest fears is public speaking (Glossophobia). To overcome this requires a very strong, centered sense of self. In order to tell the powerful story, we must come from a position of power. To effectively fight hard for our characters, we cannot be doubting ourselves. An actor who is not confident cannot do the job well.

Being confident helps us in a number of ways. We tell our story more powerfully. Our audience will be comfortable with us in the spotlight. And we will find our Actor Brain quieted, giving us freedom to swim deep in our Character Brain.

All of us as actors (and certainly those who care enough to be reading this) understand the need for discipline in our work. If we take and understanding of actor cake, we don't have to wait for the director to tell us we are good (or to prove ourselves in any way) in order to feel confident. We aren't going to feel confident in reaction to anything. We will simply feel confident because we are disciplined.

Don't wait for it. Confidence cannot be given. It can only be taken. It may feel a bit disingenuous at first. That's doesn't matter. We don't have to earn confidence. Unlike experience - we have to earn experience - confidence is there to be seized. We don't have to get permission or wait and see what the reviews say. Or what it sounds like when we go for that high note. We are simply confident because we have the discipline of a professional. We can show up confident like we show up on time - because we're disciplined.

The audience feels comfortable looking at someone who feels comfortable being looked at. That is part of the basic contract. They agreed to look at us, and we agreed to be comfortable being look at. We have to live up to our end of the deal, or else the audience will feel cheated. And rightly so.

Getting Invited to the Party

Everyone is talented. No matter how talented you are, someone else is at least as talented. There is always another actor who could play the role. Unless you're an A-list star, virtually no one is so special that the director and producers cannot do without them.

When the casting team are making their choices, whether it's a movie with a million dollar budget or a job in summer stock, they are deciding who to invite to the party. It's important to be a good party guest.

Every production is a party, one with extremely high-stakes. This is one reason it can be so difficult to break into the business. It seems all of the people in power only want to hire their friends. So would you. You know you can trust your friends to be good party guests.

When you are throwing a party, what qualities do you look for in your guests? You want someone you can count on to show up at the appropriate time. You want someone who is respectful and considerate to all the other guests. You want people who are upbeat and fun to be around. You don't want guests who are going to get drunk and cry in the corner. You don't want guests are going to hit on your wife. You don't want guests who are going to belittle or intimidate your other guests or spill red wine all over your white shag carpeting.

Casting directors always have a choice. If there are two actors for the role and they're equally talented and appropriate, the role will go to the one who's the better party guest. Make sure that is you.

We can develop the skills necessary to build a solid reputation. When we do this we can increase the likelihood of being selected for the project. In fact, in a real way, your reputation is more important than your talent.

Make everyone who works with you want to work with you again. This includes not only the casting team, but everyone associated with the production. The personnel in wardrobe, props, administrative assistants, musicians, people in the chorus and even the ushers. All of them may have a say in whether you get hired again. Make sure that no matter who it is, if they are asked if you are the right person for the job, they enthusiastically say yes. These "yeses" are building blocks for a successful career.

We see plenty of examples of directors choosing to work with the same actors repeatedly. These actors are trusted and proven in the eyes of those in charge of creating the product and deciding who to bring into the production. They choose these actors because they have confidence in them. They are proven.

To be a working actor we must develop the skills that make people want to work with us on a consistent basis. If everyone you work with wants to work with you again, acting opportunities will naturally come your way. And with a highly regarded reputation, keep coming your way.

House of Cards

Every production - whether it be a TV series or a play or a film - is in the initial stages, a house of cards. The glue is not yet dry. The foundation has not been tested. In fact, it's being constructed around us. Virtually any tremor or outburst may cause it to come crashing to the ground. All of the elements around us; crew, directors, designers, are yet to be tested against a storm. Especially at this stage of the process, be the glue that holds it together.

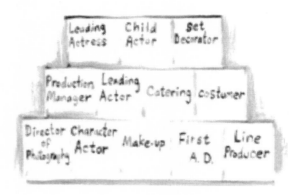

Sometimes actors fail to consider their role in this. And how certain behaviors may very well be shaking the foundation and endangering the overall structure of a production. They sometimes do this because they think they're helping or because of a feeling of self-importance or anxiety.

One behavior we should watch out for consists of playing devil's advocate or questioning the integrity of the line of dialogue or actions of our characters. That is not giving credit to the efforts of those who have crafted your material. An actor who complains "My character would never say this" is not playing the right character.

We can also be "high maintenance" actors. Having to call the production office because we don't remember what our call time is. Showing up without our scripts, or not knowing our lines. Taking time away from rehearsal explaining what you were trying to do in your scene, instead of simply taking the note the director gives you. Constantly having improvements on the scene or the dialogue. Having suggestions for how other actors should do their lines, or how they should play their characters. These rather boorish behaviors happen surprisingly often among well-meaning, talented yet inexperienced actors.

Savvy directors, producers and casting people understand that what is required in the performances and the choices they make for their cast, is to add a bonding element to the production. To strengthen what they encounter, and to not be the harsh wind that challenges the structural integrity. Many actors may have a tendency to challenge their material. Sometimes this happens because they feel that they know better than those around them. That their idea is better than the one crafted by the writing team, the other actors and the director. Don't be this actor.

It is a fragile process. Whether we are on a TV or film set, in rehearsal at our community theater or a Broadway stage, in a class or improv troupe, in the dressing room or at an audition.

Sometimes our house of cards is merely an hour of rehearsal. It doesn't take much of a breeze to knock down the structure of that hour of rehearsal. Something simple like chattiness or getting distracted or off-topic or not knowing your lines may be enough of a breeze to seriously reduce the effectiveness of that particular hour.

Producers and directors are always aware of the house of cards. Their job is to oversee its construction and supervise all aspects regarding its sturdiness and completion. They know how important it is to have the right people in place, and that each person is doing what's best for the construction of the whole project. We must be aware and sensitive to our place in this structure.

Also, in the rehearsal process, unless you are a seasoned pro, don't have ideas for characters other than our own. Don't suggest what great piece of business your scene partner might do.

The director will take care of what the other actor should do. That is the person who has been placed in charge of instructing everybody and heightening the audience's experience. In a healthy production environment, you as the actor are usually invited to have ideas for yourself and the way in which you play your role. That falls under your jurisdiction. What the other performers are doing is not part of your purview.

Everyone's ego is a house of cards. No actor can succeed in an atmosphere of fear and mistrust. If they are not confident in their performance and supported by the ensemble, their work will naturally become either subdued out of fear or forced by desperation. The healthy creative flow cannot happen when an actor is doubting their work or in fear of it how they are being judged by others. When this happens, the entire project is diminished, from the joy in everyone's efforts to the quality of the product itself.

It is embarrassing and disgraceful when actors take advantage of other people's honesty and vulnerability. Far too many oafish jerks look at the rehearsal room as a pick up joint or that it is an emotional free-for-all. Others may use it as a therapy session or a chance to assert their dominance or self-importance.

When you concentrate on holding your fellow actors up, you will help create a stronger ensemble of actors. The house of cards gets stronger. This can directly relate to you edging out another auditioner for a role. The other actor may be just as good as you are, but you support the production, help make the actors around you better and contribute to a supportive environment. I would cast you.

There is an element of trust that is so important in our work. This is a business where it might be your job to kiss or grope another actor. There's lots of people changing clothes. There's lots of vulnerability and tears. Trying and failing. We want to be sure to create an environment where actors feel free to experiment and take risks.

Help a Brother Out

We can help a brother out by dedicating our work to making the other actor look good in our scene. Not us.

To make ourselves look good in the scene is average, to help the other actors look good is exceptional, generous. So in helping a brother out, we elevate the scene and the story, not simply our own performance.

This kind of a quality is irresistible to casting directors. If an artistic director is casting for a season and they have one more slot open, one more performer to cast, they will not choose the actor who is most "talented" but the actor who is best at helping the ensemble excel. It is these actors that help make a production excellent. They are the glue that holds the house of cards together and they do it selflessly.

We need a healthy sense of confidence to take this approach. We are behaving confidently when we work to support and elevate the other performances instead of our own.

How do we do this? We might consider ourselves as the fuel that helps the other performer burn brighter. By exploiting the opportunities they are presenting. We can also give focus to the other actor, so that the spotlight is placed on their work at crucial moments, only taking the spotlight back when it is our dramatic turn.

It may seem obvious to you in the anonymity of reading this book, but it's amazing how often we see this type of scenario - one actor may have the line, "Calm down." and yet the other actor has given them nothing to react to in saying this line. Help a Brother Out. Give them a reason to say what they have to say to or about you.

If you see after your character exits that someone says, "That's the meanest person I ever met," Help a Brother Out. Give them a reason to say that line. Don't leave that actor hanging who has to say "Calm down" - don't leave him hanging if his line is "Stop laughing." Don't leave someone hanging if she has to say later how scared she was of you. Provide soil for this dramatic revelation. Help a Brother Out.

When the other character is speaking we can help a brother out by being interested in what they say. The other character in the scene can't be scary if you're not scared. The other character can't be inspiring if you're not inspired. Help a Brother Out.

Of course by selflessly helping our fellow performers to their best work, we also get something out of it. The indirect benefit is that by being generous to others, we are also showing ourselves in our best light. The audience will find this generosity of spirit equally attractive and powerful, and so will the creative team. By directing the spotlight to the other person we are playing with, we put ourselves in a favorable light as well.

Under-acting

How many times have you left your audition thinking that you fell short of what you had envisioned for your read? It is quite often the fear of over-acting that causes us to give such a subdued performance. Of course to indulge yourself in your emotions is indeed over-acting. But a much more common problem is under-acting.

Under-acting manifests itself quite easily. Auditions are scary. And we certainly don't want to get caught over-acting. Perhaps we have heard time and time again that stage actors (where our background is) are too large for camera. So we constantly try to tone it down to the point where many high-quality actors do virtually nothing with the opportunities the text has given them.

Directors know that it's much easier to get an actor to *tone down* their performance, than it is to *pull an actor up* to the performance they want.

Most of us don't need to fear over-acting. Instead let's develop a nice healthy fear of under-acting. Let's develop a fear of missed opportunities, small stakes, and reasonable character behavior.

This note often applies to more advanced actors. People who have studied a long time, perhaps have a college degree, or lots of credits. It may also apply to those who have the most appreciation of the art form itself. Quite often, this perspective leads us to place the work of being an actor in a Glass Museum in the Sky.

The Glass Museum in the Sky is all the brilliant performances and actors that have come before you. The ones that inspired you; great broadway stars, movie stars, virtuosos.

Actors with drive and passion have an appreciation for the finest acting. Yet sometimes we don't believe in ourselves because we haven't achieved what the greats have achieved and that our work is no good in comparison. That we'll never live up to our expectations.

This can cause actors (even those with lots of good training, instincts, and in some cases years of experience) to lose confidence in themselves. We may underachieve because of this point of view. Sometimes we quit. The saddest part is that it's usually the most deserving and humble actors that this happens to.

We don't have to live up to anyone's standards, instead we have the opportunity to create new standards. If it was easy, everyone would do it. We won't be fully expressed in our work unless we obliterate this glass museum and realize it was never in the sky in the first place, it was merely our perception.

Bring the glass museum down to earth and smash the hell out of it. Stomp it. Break it. There's nothing to attain, there's no one we have to live up to or be as good as. We don't have to compare our work to anything. It's fine to have an appreciation for the masters that have come before us, but it becomes disempowering when we create an unreachable standard for ourselves. Many extremely talented actors can be virtually crippled by this. In most cases those are the actors who deserve to have the most confidence in their work. Because of the passion they bring and their high standards.

The Glass Museum is unreasonably sacred and untouchable... unattainable. To be viewed, but from a distance. We cannot have ownership of a glass museum. We're treating the objects with too much reverence. We're actors too. We can applaud and appreciate those who have gone before us and our peers, but there's no need to put anyone on a pedestal, past or present. To do that creates a barrier - keeping us from what it is we're admiring.

Don't let the thing we strive for become unattainable because of our admiration for it. Let's move that self-imposed barrier out of the way.

Audition Perspective

The more we want the job, the more nerves we may encounter. If we can look at the big acting jobs and think of them as little acting jobs, we can counter those nerves. Try this mantra:

"I'm probably going to turn this job down, but It's nice to meet everyone."

Especially in a big audition, bring a bit of that "I'm probably going to turn this job down" mentality to help bring the audition down to your level. Bring the "...but it's nice to meet everyone" as well so you don't come off as aloof. The point is not that you want to work with them, it's to make them want to work with you,

It's a lot like in a courtship. If you go on a first date with someone and they start talking about getting married, you will be turned off. You can sense the desperation. Don't be the one proposing marriage on a first date. Take the time for you and the casting team to woo each other.

Over the course of an actor's career, there will be jobs that the actor will turn down. Certainly if you're in one of the unions, you will turn down non-union work. Or once you've played at the big regional theater, you might not choose to perform at the local amateur playhouse. Really, how high up the ladder you are, is determined by how many rungs are below you. Ultimately, your career is defined by the jobs you turn down.

When we are first starting out, (you - by nature of reading this book - are somewhere on the ladder) we are happy to take virtually any job we are offered. We are happy for the experience even though there is no pay and long hours. We are glad to do it because at least we are on the ladder. And for a period of time it will be quite an accomplishment to simply be on the ladder at all.

This is necessary and exactly as it should be. It takes time to get your footing. To understand how to balance and not fall or get knocked off. The best actors work on acting everyday. There is no shortcut to experience. You have to earn it.

Tip:

To use a sports analogy, you may want to keep track of "wins and losses." It isn't only a win to be "cast" in the production you may be auditioning for. Instead it's a win to be "strongly considered." If you are strongly considered often enough, you'll get your share of roles.

"Wins" are anytime you're cast, called back, or feel you had a good audition. The only "losses" are when you feel you didn't do your best. If you have 2 auditions, - one good and you're cast and one bad and you're not cast - That's one win for a good audition, one win for getting cast and one loss for a bad audition. Two wins and one loss. By redefining winning and losing, we can find a more empowering gauge for our career.

Stand Next to the Camera

What is on the screen is what they want the audience to see. To fool them. As magicians, we can't be fooled by the Magic Trick. When watching films or television don't merely look at the screen and let yourself be fooled. Stand next to the camera.

If you (pretend to) stand next to the camera you are on the set of what you're watching. You are aware of the practical elements involved in producing it: the crew, lighting equipment, the wardrobe and makeup department. They are all present. If we stand next to the camera, we can stop being fooled by the magic trick and figure out how they did it.

FTP

In the contract between you and your audience, the audience agrees you will be in charge.

Nervousness is one of the most common and disempowering aspects to actors in their work. Nerves happen to almost every actor in almost any medium at almost any event. It's possible to feel nerves anywhere. They are very prevalent in the audition room and on opening night.

It is natural that we'd feel nervous when in front of an audience. One of the greatest fears in the world is public speaking. Some studies have suggested that people are statistically more afraid of public speaking than they are of death.

There is a mantra for each of us to use anytime we are we feeling nervous in anticipation of a big audition or performance. The phrase to repeat in your head is, "Fuck these people."

Literally try taking this mantra on. Anytime you're feeling nervous, a presentation at school, a scene in class, opening night, an audition – bring this mantra with you. It is virtually impossible to think FTP and be nervous at the same time. Consider it the Big Nerves Eliminator and it's practical and easy.

It's important that the audience not see this, but we can use it to empower our perspective. If we have disdain for our audience, we won't be concerned with how they may judge us. By using this approach, you are taking their power away. And giving it back to you.

We're casting our audience as first graders and we are the teacher. We're not going to ask for their permission or approval to lead them. The first grade teacher's job is to instruct, empower and enlighten their audience. We can't pander to the audience's preconceptions or expectations. The point is for them to grow because of their experience with us, to be challenged, to learn. We're not there to be liked.

FTP is an aspect of star quality, the it factor, charisma. It can be benevolent and loving. We aren't bad people because we use FTP. After all, we use it to get past our nerves and empower us to tell loving stories. Nervousness will derail our work if we let it.

Imagine auditioning for a top Hollywood director. When you walk into the room you'll be nervous and hoping to please. You'll be hoping they like you as much you like them. In this scenario, with so much at stake, we are likely to blow the opportunity.

If we can walk into the same opportunity with an FTP mindset, the director will see us not as another actor who needs a job but as a peer, a fellow artist. Directors want to work with actors who will inspire and motivate them as well, who are equally or more talented. They don't need someone who is awe-struck or eager to please.

Fuck These People is an Actor Brain mantra. We use it specifically to overcome nerves, the bigger the job the more we might bring it. But don't forget the Ace of Clubs. Don't let the auditor (or audience) see this card up your sleeve. Just FTP so that you're empowered to do the work the best you can do and not try to please everyone else.

Some people don't like the "F" word. I use it because of my commitment to how much I don't care about pleasing my audience. I am unreasonably committed to not pleasing you, while greeting with a "Hi, lovely to meet you." If we have that kind of balance, we've got something to offer other than an actor who's hoping to please everybody and get a paycheck.

They are looking for an expert on the role you're playing. If you have had 15 minutes in the lobby with the scene, consider yourself the expert, not the author, not the director, you. You've spent 15 minutes, you're living it. The director has read it, the writer wrote it, but you are living it. Now you are the expert.

If you've had a day or a week, then it's even more true. On opening night of Cat on a Hot Tin Roof, there is one expert in that building on Maggie and that is you. You are living as Maggie. Same thing goes for the audition. The auditors are not the experts, you are. Of course we're going to make the adjustments and take notes and we're not a know-it-all, but right now in this room I'm the one living this role. What you hope I do isn't part of my equation. You're only watching. I'm actually living it.

Of course, we are loving people. This is a big Ace of Clubs. If anybody ever sees this FTP part of our magic trick we will blow the illusion terribly. It's just our secret.

Fight or Flight

We humans have a gland in our brains called the hypothalamus. (The area I am referring to is actually a series of glands) All mammals have this. It causes what is called a "fight or flight impulse." It is present in all of us and very powerful. It sends primal impulses coursing through our bodies. It is the adrenaline rush that can give us power and energy to run faster than we have ever run before or even in some cases be able to lift an automobile to save a life.

When we experience the pressure of an audition or an opening night, our hypothalamus switches into overdrive. This gland is screaming at you "Ruuuuun! This is scary, let's get the hell out of here!" This causes your voice to quiver, your hand to shake, little beads of sweat on your forehead. This is your brain hurling you into survival mode.

Choose Fight. When we tell our hippocampus to turn away from Flight and instead turn to Fight, everything changes. We turn into Momma Bear. Momma Bear isn't scared or nervous. She will defend her cubs at any cost. Tune into that primal response. Instead of the disempowering experience of being nervous, we tune into the very empowering experience of attack. When we tell our hypothalamus to turn away from Flight and instead turn to Fight, everything changes.

Our brains and bodies respond with a rush of testosterone. Our fear turns to passion. Instead of doubting ourselves, we defend our point of view. And when we vigorously defend our personal point of view, we tap into what is most unique and powerful about ourselves.

Of Course

Use this as a mantra anytime the pressure is high. It helps us not be overwhelmed in overwhelming situations. It provides confidence and overcomes nerves and doubt.

Since what we do is one of the scariest things in the world, "of course" helps us get that equilibrium back. Without that balance we might be in varying states of panic, our heart and mind racing.

Nervousness may actually be the repetition of the mantra "Oh my God, oh my God." So our disempowered processing comes out like this:

(rapid) OMG, it's opening night, OMG, there's a critic in the audience, OMG, everyone's watching, OMG, there are people out there, OMG, my parents are here, OMG, everyone's counting on me. OMG, OMG.

For most of us this and this would be terribly disempowering. Even if we feel we have it under control to some degree, (omg, omg) it is detracting from our power.

Similarly to fight or flight impulse, we have the opportunity to make the empowered choice:

(slow) Of course it's opening night, Of course there's a critic in the audience, Of course everyone's watching, Of course there are people out there, Of course my parents are here, Of course everyone's counting on me. Of course. Of course.

I do not have to stand in awe of the event, nor do I have to pretend in denial. I consider myself to be more than equal to the task. Of course I am.

Of course I have an audition. Of course I get this opportunity. Of course the audience is laughing.

Of Course reminds us that nothing unusual is happening. We are simply very effective at what we do. What we do is relevant enough that lots of people - sometimes important people like casting directors, audiences and critics - are going to see us at work. Of course they are.

Toning it Down For the Camera

Many stage actors are intimidated by on camera acting. Don't be. While there are differences, there are only a few. Effective acting works in both places.

For most stage actors, the main adjustment has to do with speaking volume. It's that simple. Stage actors are taught to hit the back row, to fill the room with their voices. In on camera work the microphone is just out of the shot or hidden in your costume. You no longer need to fill the room with your voice. Let the microphone do its job. You only have to project as far as the actor you are speaking to in the scene with you, no further.

In this setting the microphone also offers an opportunity to create intimacy with your audience. You can speak softly, introspectively. This can draw the audience's ear toward you, cause them to lean in, giving them a sense of intimacy with your character. By speaking softly you are drawing them in and sending a message that this is an intimate and even private moment.

You still need vocal and verbal energy however. Just because you're speaking softly doesn't mean you should communicate less vibrantly. Don't let this idea give you the excuse to be lazy in your diction. When speaking softly you should energize your diction even more. This equation is true of stage as well. As the volume comes down the ratio of verbal energy comes up.

Most actors have heard their whole careers that stage actors are too large for film. This can cause excellent stage actors to shut down in front of the camera. Their choices and execution can become tentative. Their faces and bodies can become rigid. They fear anything they do will be over-acting.

We still need to tell our stories powerfully. The scrutiny of the camera can't get in our way. We are used to communicating to the back row but now the audience is a camera lens a few feet away. How do we handle this adjustment?

As the audience gets closer, we need to raise the failure in our communication. We should become less efficient. Our words and our thoughts need to differ more. Keep the stakes high but let the character's doubts and uncertainties rise.

The intimacy of the camera dictates that we fail more. The camera will catch you if you succeed. As we know that is bad magic. We must invite more failure because of the intense scrutiny of the camera. Employ a larger dose of Anti-Acting.

Stage is more of a "Succeed" medium. It has to be. Because of the distance between you and your audience. To communicate effectively to the back row means we must succeed more. As that back row moves closer - that is the distance you need to communicate - we invite more failure.

It is similar to the difference between playing a 2000 seat theater and a 49 seat theater. In the larger venue you must succeed more. The back row will not see the point without a larger measure of succeed. In the smaller venue, the distance you need to communicate becomes less. Perhaps the back row is just 20 feet away from you. You don't need to cover the distance in a large venue, so you can invite more failure.

The camera is often within 2 or 3 feet of your face. Even when the camera is further away they may have zoomed in to an intimate look. Instead of the audience being a grand hall, it is a 3 inch wide lens a couple of feet away from you. If you succeed in this scenario the same way you succeed in the large venue, you will be caught over-acting.

We don't want the camera to intimidate us into telling small stories. Our audience is much closer but our responsibility to tell a bold story is just as relevant as ever. Just because you are failing more doesn't mean your story should become tentative or the experience less powerful.

Isn't This Fun?

... reminds us of a playful approach to our material, and perhaps a hint of mischief underneath. Comedy almost always has an element of isn't this fun. Isn't this fun? reminds us to create an environment of openness, warmth and unreasonableness. Most comedic performers will have this in their natural personalities.

Bring isn't this fun? with you into the room. We all like to hang out with our fun friends. So does our audience. We like to be in places where we are having fun, other people are having fun. If the experience of watching us perform is fun, it is already satisfying.

Your fun friends entertain you. Simply have your fun friend arrive at your door, and you're already having fun.

They keep you guessing. You're having fun in anticipation of having fun. You will go out of your way for it. Wasn't that a fun paragraph?

There is an irresistible quality to someone who is having fun. It's a fundamental characteristic of people who have charisma. Charm. Apply it in both Actor Brain and Character Brain.

In Actor Brain:

A positive outlook will make us more desirable to be around. It helps the casting people and production team believe we will be an asset to their project. Not to the degree where we become silly or push our attitude onto others, but as a supportive and upbeat member of the team. Someone who looks forward to going to work every day.

Use isn't this fun? to get invested in your character's world. To enjoy the process of being spontaneous while telling a powerful story. Acting is actually a game we play. To enjoy the process will help us excel at it.

It is also a trap to take ourselves too seriously. Actors who take themselves too seriously are harming the process. Sometimes, directors are reluctant to give them notes, because it may throw the actor into a funk. Often for these self-important actors, any criticism from the director will cause them to shut down and start to shatter their fragile confidence.

Isn't this fun? helps the director understand you can handle whatever needs to be said. The director then can take an honest approach. Directors prefer to work with actors to whom they can communicate openly. Don't be an actor that causes a director to become careful.

Avoid too much laughter. It can come across as nervousness and fake. Take note that the phrase is "Isn't this fun?," not "I'm having fun." Always make sure they are laughing more than you. If you are the one laughing the most, you've got this equation wrong.

Often the stress of being an actor can make us forget that underneath it all, it's supposed to be fun. Whether it is an actor who is enjoying the process of being an actor or a character who enjoys being their character. Even in drama. The audience is drawn to watching people who are having fun, even if we're having fun being despondent.

This translates to other genres as well. Glamorous movie stars of yesteryear had isn't this fun? in spades. Katharine Hepburn would be a prime example of this. That mischievous gleam in the eyes tells an isn't this fun? story. The result is flirtatious, fiery, glamorous, giving her characters consistent sex appeal. Isn't this fun? is a natural part of sex appeal. George Clooney certainly has it. And why wouldn't he? I'll bet it's fun to be George Clooney.

In Character Brain:

A positive aspect of isn't this fun? in our character brain, is that our audiences will enjoy being around us. They will seek us out. It will make us a destination. It will make us easy to root for by bringing positivity and spontaneity to our work.

If we use this as a mantra, it will set the tone for an audience to find their way to laughter. Sitcom performances will usually have an element of this. The underlying message to our audience is "you are seeing me at work. Isn't this fun?" Or "I am at the end of my rope. Isn't this fun?" In a practical sense, at your audition you can simply say to yourself "I just walked into the room. Isn't this fun?"

In comedy, use this mantra when your character is angry. Comedy has a delicate balance and to keep the audience's mind at ease, use isn't this fun? Let your character be angry, but make them terrible at it. Great comedians (Dick Van Dyke again) in situation comedies use isn't this fun? when playing that angry dad. The character can threaten another character, but the audience must know that the threat is benign in order to laugh. If they think that your character is dangerous, it will add a level of seriousness that can dampen the audience's laugh reflex. There can be exceptions however, as in "dark comedy," where this danger works well.

Isn't this fun? is a direct conduit to comedy. But it can also add contrast and weight to the dramatic moment. Characters who face adversity but don't wallow in self-pity, are helping the audience to invest in their futures.

And certainly don't forget this aspect when working in commercials. It can be a fundamental part of selling a product.

Falling In Love

Most often, when an actor cannot identify with their character it is because they have not yet fallen in love. They see their characters as blasé, uninteresting. It is also quite common for actors to judge the characters that they play negatively. Don't fall into this trap. Don't be dismissive of the characters that you play.

Our characters are faced with difficult choices, have a hard time making the right decision, and often choose wrongly. We do not write screenplays about average people doing average things. The very nature of dramatic tension requires a lot be at stake. Because of this dynamic, often our characters behave in ways that seem ugly or desperate. They might behave in ways that we never would.

Avoid the temptation to judge your character. Your character's flaws are more interesting than their positive qualities. Don't hide their flaws or fix your characters. Instead, take advantage of how they are broken.

At work or in the classroom we have opportunities like crazy to fall in love. Let's completely put aside any ideas of sex or romance, this is just love. Every time we act in an environment with creative types, look for the opportunity to fall in love, with the project, the people, the mission. Fall in love with the language of your text, fall in love with your author. Fall in love with your co-star, your stage manager, your director. In all of our work, find an active, loving approach.

I'm not suggesting you give everybody shoulder rubs (don't, it's creepy) but to fall in love with the process and all the people participating in the process. This idea of falling in love can make us more fun to work with, develop lifelong friendships, provide a selfless and loving community for yourself and your fellow artists and make great art. If we contribute in that way to our productions, we are going to be very valuable to people who are looking to hire actors or work in any environment.

This is most so in the creative world. Done with a great deal of maturity, of course, we can see that this is fundamentally our job. And this can add in every way to the quality of the experience. It can make those around you better. It makes you better. It helps the director to achieve greater heights.

Of course, most of us do this. We're good people, active and loving. (I give you a lot of credit for reading this book.) It's not enough to assume this will happen in our work because we're good people. This is our job as a professional. That is what is going to give the people who invest in us, Producers and Directors and Casting Directors - bosses of every kind - more value in our work. This becomes our reputation. Again, our reputation is more important than our talent.

In society, actors play the role of those who point the way toward love. Actors lead the way toward a better tomorrow in the roles they play. Ultimately, everything is about love. What is To Kill a Mockingbird but love? hat is E.T. but love? What is The Diary of Anne Frank but love?

Actors must be in touch with love to every degree possible. We will look to become the vessel or messenger of that love. It's there in every story. To do our jobs well is to identify, heighten and bring love. Of course sometimes the powerful story would be in its denial. To tell the story of denial of love powerfully we need to identify the love to our work so that its denial is a large dramatic event.

A lot of actor training seems to put actors in a state of grief. Take an average actor, flip the switch and say "it's time to act" and they will immediately begin exploring anger, grief, despair. Let's let our neutral state of being choose love.

In a scene, if your character needs to cry, try using beauty, not despair. Beauty is much more accessible and watchable, it doesn't have the morbidity that actors may have as a default setting. Let's emotionally charge our scenes with beauty and love and not default towards despair and grief.

When the audience experiences a character filled with love or when a producer meets an actor filled with love - either way - they're more likely to care about what happens. More likely to root for you, to look forward to seeing you again, to look forward to spending time with you.

Falling in love with our characters is fundamental to fighting hard for them. We cannot fight hard for someone we disapprove of. Find a way to love your character, despite their flaws, and give the audience an opportunity to do the same.

In some cases the powerful story is about a character that is quite unlovable. Maybe a villain, dictator, etc. In these cases the loving story is not demonstrated by the character we're playing. In fact, our character is demonstrating the opposite of love so we can illuminate the call to action towards love.

Usually the character's powerful story will come out of what's lovable about the character. The audience will be more invested in characters if they find them lovable. We can find our characters lovable even if we don't personally approve of their actions.

Whether it's as an actor or as a character. People like love.

Taking Good Shots

Training the way an athlete prepares is a good example for us. Before we decide specifically which sport (theatre, film, musicals or whatever) we become excellent athletes. Then we apply the appropriate skills to the sport we've been selected to play.

Ultimately it's not about the medium but becoming the best athlete, so that whether we're called upon to play the sport of comedy or drama, we excel at both because we're well trained. We build our instincts like an athlete builds muscles.

Our instincts are the result of a lot of training. We hear and then understand concepts in acting, but they do not become our instincts until much later. At first, we can't lift the weight, then our muscles hurt when we lift the weight but eventually, we can lift the weight without having to try.

There's a level of humility in sports as well that is very important. Kobe Bryant is on anybody's list of the greatest basketball players to ever play in the NBA. Note that during his career, when Kobe shot the basketball, it went in the basket about 45% of the time. One of the greatest players of all time - Kobe Bryant - missed more often than he made his shots!

Let's understand that my job as an actor is to take good shots and I can't worry about whether they go into the net or not. I'm not going to be worried about results, I'm just going to take good shots, what I think are high percentage shots. I can't force the ball to go in.

In baseball the best hitters only get a hit about a third of the time. Most of the time they make outs. But each time they come up there is a very real potential for a hit.

Something exciting may happen... but is never guaranteed. If it were guaranteed there would be no suspense.

In acting, that is the risk of playing the game at all. If 100% of our shots go in, we're playing on a children's basket with no defense. If 100% of the time we hit a home run, the fence is too close. If we hit a bull's eye 100% of the time we're standing right next to the target. Move the target further away. And then make it dance. Now, there is something at stake. We have to take the risk of missing it, for it to be eventful when we hit it.

Juggling

When I was a kid, I taught myself to juggle and now see juggling as a helpful metaphor for acting. The balls are the techniques we use. We have to decide which are needed at which time. No one can juggle all of them at once. Because every situation (i.e. style, story, role, line) will be unique, the instincts we develop will help us decide when to put this ball down and pick that one up. We cannot control the air currents, gravity or surroundings. In order to keep the balls in the air, we will acknowledge and react to their natural power.

The juggler will be imperfect. Each ball will peak with a slightly unpredictable arc. Each will have a variety of spins. When we catch them, they will hit our hand somewhat differently. These nuances are part of juggling. They're to be expected and welcome.

We can't cling to one or two techniques. Our instincts tell us to choose several, take a chance and let them fly. We have to risk dropping one. We can't juggle if we aren't willing to fail.

Summary

Telling stories is as fundamental a human right as food or shelter. All human beings have a right to tell stories. Keeping that in mind, it's okay if we're not the best storyteller ever, I still have the right to do it. In this relationship that we're discussing between ourselves and ourselves in the role of performer, it's good to know that even as a beginner I have a right to try; to audition, to find a class, to explore, to develop my skills. We all have the fundamental ability to be actors, because to be actors is to be human.

When I was younger I used to hear the expression "to walk a mile in someone else's shoes." Actors do this as a way of life. They actively inquire into what it is like to be someone else. I think it is fundamentally the most noble of pursuits. It is compassion in action.

The actor gives voice to those who are not there to speak for themselves. They are surrogates for common people. They fight injustice, reward heroism, make us root for the underdog and show us the beauty in the seemingly mundane.

They bravely let us see what others would hide. This provides an outlet for those who attend our performances. So that I, in the audience, understand I'm not the only one who feels the way I do. Even in my loneliest moments, I am not alone. Even when I feel my most unlovable, I am loved. Someone understands me. Actors provide this as a sort of public-service.

Taken further, acting is really a study in love. Sometimes the story takes us to the place where we are in denial of love. Or the story is the quest for love. Love is the most powerful emotion and all other emotions are simply a response to it. What is anger but fear of losing love?

Often the love we discover through this inquiry, is the love of self. A better understanding of our place in our world gives us a more charitable view toward ourselves and those around us. To play a role is to look at the world from a viewpoint other than your own. To walk a mile in your characters shoes. This gives us perspective on our own lives. Actors spend their lives doing this. We are advanced students of being human, with a major in communication.

When the love is heightened and communicated powerfully in our work, we can bring about tremendous change in our audiences. We can find the love in the material and then point the audience's way to it. These profound examples for our audience, can cause them to, in ways small and large, be more aware of the love available to them and the love they can create. To become a better friend. To become a better parent or brother or sister. Fight against injustice. See the similarities between people. Hear the other side of the story.

The reputation actors have for being on the liberal side of social issues is well-earned. In Hollywood, it is difficult to think of more than a couple of actors or directors who are socially conservative. When you spend your life walking miles in other people's shoes, it is quite natural that you would adopt sympathy toward their points of view.

This seems to be a genetic trait. Actors think and behave compassionately toward those with no voice because they have walked in their shoes. It is the fundamental building block of acting itself. And it works both ways. People become actors because they're compassionate, and they become more compassionate because they're actors.

Actor's WorkHouse Technique

Abrupt and Often. Changing our minds abruptly, often and with great contrast, can help us keep ourselves in a state of surprise. Secondly, asking actors to employ A&O, forces them to confront the next thought because they must change their mind. Then they realize "in relation to what?" Forces them to find a visual truth. Another benefit is that a sentence, which may seem like 1 thought, becomes about 5 thoughts. Or more.

Ace of Clubs. Part of the magic trick. The AoC is that card up your sleeve (technique) Do the trick but never let the audience see you do it. That is not good magic. When an actor employs a good choice or technique, this note reminds them to do the trick, but don't get caught doing it.

Actor Brain. The thoughts of the actor. Often disempowering. "I'm nervous." "They won't hire me." "I said that line wrong." "I hope I do a good job acting." "Cross stage right." "Ignore the camera." etc. Blocking and memorization are also Actor Brain. We need it. Actor Brain was at rehearsal.

Actor Cake. "Confidence is to the actor, what flour is to the cake. There are sprinkles, icing, food coloring, but your cake is made of confidence. That is what we are made of." b.) "Don't be confident because of compliments or outside influence. Have confidence because it's your job." "You show up confident like you show up on time. Because you're a professional." "Don't wait to be confident later." (empowering)

Actor Motor. Tightly wound. Hyped up. OMGOMGOMGOMG. Aware of their "big moment" (Actor Brain) and trying to overcome nerves and insecurity. Symptoms include rushing pace, stiffness, and success orientation.

Aggressive Act. The conscious intention to create dramatic action. Creating discomfort.

Anti-Acting. Avoiding doing what actors do. Helps actors do it "wrong." Actors "make sense, look good, say it good, keep going, try to please, try to be believable, Let's NOT do that."

Answer to Every Question. "Whatever will best serve the audience's experience." Not whatever is logical, emotional, feels good, etc.

Arrows. Arrows indicate dramatic movement. Flow, expectation, resolve, etc. Arrows move away from our unit (the line, the scene, the role) and explore what is possible in opposition to the unit. Longer arrows equal greater dramatic tension/release.

Aunt Enid. Giving extra verbal energy to "surprise words."

Call To Action. How we want our audience to be changed. Making the world a better place. Present in every satisfying piece of art. Find it. Use it.

Capital K. To *know* what you (character brain) are talking about. Using video to create (intimate, specific) knowledge. Otherwise, you literally "don't know what you are talking about."

Character Brain. The memories and thoughts of the character. Taking on their first-person point of view. In performance, we are striving for 90% Character Brain.

Comparisons. "To be or not to be" is the single greatest line of dialogue ever written in the English language. Why? Comparison, of the two furthest (highest stakes) opposing ideas (being and not being) in the most succinct possible phrase (economy) "Is love dramatically relevant in a world without hate?" Advanced actors: Lines are always more powerful when compared to everything that is *not* said.

Contrast. "Contrast tells a Powerful Story." When we contrast one moment to another, we are creating an event. Not just another line of dialogue. Greater contrast (before/after, either/or) makes events larger.

Diving Into Character Brain. Consciously deciding to think what the character is thinking. (First Person Memory) This helps actors "get out of their heads" and fight for the character, not the actor.

Don't Let What You Say Dictate How You Say It.

Economy of Movement. Stripping away movements that do not tell the powerful story. All movement that does not enhance the performance is weakening the performance. Through EoM, the audience gets to zoom in for a close-up. Present an in-focus picture, not a blurry one.

Events. Things that happen to your character, or in the scene. Not just story (falls in love, wins the lottery) but also whenever we go from here to there. To suddenly become suspicious, anxious, relieved, get an idea, come to a decision... Providing events for our audience. When people talk about what a good time they had, they'll say "this happened, then this happened." Not "they said this and then said this."

Every Actor, All the Time. "Discover what is possible, not what is there."

Failing. A good thing. Embracing the inherent untruth of words. In general terms "succeed" in the powerful story moment and fail before and after. (contrast)

Fighting Hard. Raising the stakes for our character. Identifying what the character is fighting for, (their point of view) and taking on their fight (first person) with a vengeance.

Fight Harder for the Character Than You are Fighting for Yourself. Helps an actor "lose himself" in a role. Gets the "actor" out of the room, so the character is left. Helps overcome nerves (which are actor brain) and guides the actor toward thinking character thoughts (empowering) instead of actor thoughts (usually disempowering.) A good part of the magic trick.

Find Out. An empowered approach to "listening." Listening is "ear acting." Finding out is listening with your heart, gut.

First Person Memory. The characters point of view. "**Think** what the character thinks, **See** what the character sees, **Remember** what the character remembers. Want what the character wants. Fear what the character fears. Right now, real time." Having the character's memory, instead of *looking* like you have the character's memory.

FTP. "Fuck these people." A great cure for nerves. Takes power away from your audience and gives it to you. Even at your audition. FTP "Nice to meet you Mr Spielberg." FTP "Thank you for the opportunity." FTP.

Gilligan Effect. The worst possible person for the job. Sailor? Gilligan. Bedside manner? Dr. House. Deputy? Barney Fife. Boss? Michael Scott. Running for office? Alcoholic. In love with the popular girl? Unpopular. Creating a huge dramatic obstacle for your character to overcome. If your character does overcome, it is a much larger event.

If It Feels Good, Don't Do It. An antidote for overacting. Helps us avoid indulging ourselves in emotion (character brain) and kick-ass performance (actor brain) Reminding ourselves to change our minds. Stay surprised.

Impolite Story. The polite story is never the powerful story.

Intimate Glimpse. Letting the audience in on your character's secret. Confiding in your audience deepens their bond with you.

Isn't This Fun? Use in Actor Brain, Character Brain, auditions, all comedy and even drama. In Actor Brain, "Isn't this fun to be an actor? "I just entered, Isn't this fun?" In Character Brain, "Isn't this fun to see me frustrated?" (Everybody Loves Raymond) Anger will kill comedy without ITF. Even find a way to bring it into heavy drama. Avoids morbidity.

Leading Tone. A musical reference. Two and seven in the scale. (In the key of C, D is two and B is seven) Creates tension in the listener. Expectation. Intentionally using leading tone can keep the audience's ear awake, and in an expectation/ tension (of resolve/release)

Life Event. Look for the opportunity to present a moment in our characters lives, where we will never be the same. The entire future trajectory of your character is changed in this moment. The audience is glad to see a life event, and will feel intimacy with your character. Part of Powerful Story.

Line-sayer. Some actors are good line-sayers. Sounding like the character, but without truth. These actors need to Shoot the Video. "Let the video say the line."

Magic Trick. Making the audience believe that we are not actors at all, but the characters we are playing. Also, note it is not magic (actor-centric.) but a magic trick (audience-centric) "If you could make me forget you are an actor, here in this green classroom, and make me think I am in 17th century Bolivia, wouldn't that be the Best Magic Trick?" "Become a good magician." "The magician is not fooled. He knows there is a rabbit in the hat. He put it there before they opened the house!"

Mantra. Where we dive when we "Dive in to Character Brain." "I'm so lonely," "I hope I win," "I gotta quit this job." Mantras can change through the scene. When we find ourselves stuck in Actor Brain, Mantras are the pool we'll dive into. A conduit to Character Brain.

Navigating Our Waters. To control the ocean is false. The ocean (life) is far too powerful to control. This approach acknowledges the uncertainty of being alive. Our characters are simply trying to get home (through choppy waters) Not in control of the currents.

(the) Need to Communicate. If you see a child in danger, automatically your need to communicate will rise. "Get. Away. From. There. Right. Now." Suddenly stakes are higher, projection and diction improves. (from a character brain, empowered perspective)

Ninety-Ten. In performance this is the target ratio: 90% Character Brain, 10% Actor Brain. "We need Actor Brain. Actor Brain was at rehearsal." Certain scenarios will cause an exception to 60-40 or even 50-50. Not always a bad thing. (technique, complex physical business, fight scenes, other adjustments are all Actor Brain) Read-thru: 90% Actor Brain. Rehearse. Performance: 90% Character Brain.

One, Two, Pineapple. The reason comedy comes in threes. One establishes the thing, Two creates expectation. Pineapple is (virtually) the opposite of what was expected. Every joke is one, two, pineapple (expectation/surprise) To heighten the impact of pineapple, go back and create an expectation (1,2) that is as opposed as possible to what then becomes pineapple. "There's NO WAY I'm going camping. There's NO WAY I'm going camping!" Cut to: Camping.

Opposing Idea. A tool used to create/heighten dramatic tension. Bringing the opposite of what appears to be, with you in the line/scene. The line "I love you" said lovingly has no dramatic tension. It takes on relevance, resonance, repercussions, weight, etc,, when juxtaposed with an opposing idea (hate, jealousy, a threat, a reminder, a plea, etc) The basic unit that creates dramatic tension.

Pauses. There are 2 kinds of productive pauses:

1.) Reflective. In this pause the audience reflects on what you just said. They are having an active experience. They may be "Amen, That's so true, I agree, That's BS." It empowers what was said (and gives them ownership of their experience). Resolve tension, then pause. Reflective pause is to be used most often, giving weight to what *was* said.

2.) Anticipatory. In this pause the audience is in anticipation of what you are going to say. "The killer is.....The BUTLER" Use leading tone before the pause. This gives power to what is said after the pause. Raise tension, then pause. Use this type of pause rarely, to give weight to what *will be* said.

Plant Your Flag. Defending your emotional and physical choice. Defending your territory (point of view) This is in the moment immediately following a moment. Don't back down. Stay with it. "If after the moment, we retreat, then it never really happened." "I dare you ..."

Powerful Story. The story that affects the audience most profoundly (yet appropriately)

Powerfully Off-Balance. This is the holy grail of acting. To be powerful yet not knowing. To live in a state of surprise while effectively telling the powerful story.

Pretend So Hard. Comes from "Pretend so hard, that you (and we) are no longer in this classroom (audition room, green screen, bare stage, theatre, soundstage) but wherever you take us." Overcomes disempowering situations, environments. Part of Aggressive Act.

Self-Direct. To take on the role of director in our own work. If we do a good job self-directing, we can come closest to the directors vision for the role. "We can't wait to be directed. That happens after we're cast. If we self-direct well, it might get us the role and a chance to be directed." Ultimately, self-directing becomes your instincts. (and vice versa)

Sherlock Holmes. Looking for clues in the script. Clues are opportunities.

Shoot the Video. Creating a specific visual history. "Everywhere we have ever been, everything we have ever wanted, if it's truthful, we have a video." The video is the one rule we never break, regardless of style or other factors. The truth is in the video. Let the video say the lines.

Square Mile of Ocean. We cannot (and should not try to) control our waters (emotions, thoughts) They cannot be recreated, manipulated, or forced into place. Each moment (line, performance, take) is new and unique, like a snowflake.

State of Not Knowing. Good magic. The illusion (even to ourselves) that we do not know (the line, the scene, the response, the blocking, what to feel)

Style. Fluid. Style is present in all our work. Be pro-active in understanding style. "The actor who gets the job will be the actor who best understands and embraces style." They are varied and nuanced. One new style: "Americana." Good people trying desperately to do the right thing.

Succeed Moment. When your words and gut are in perfect alignment. Illustrated in the line "Don't go." Succeed rarely. Succeed in contrast to failing. Use succeed in the powerful story moments.

Swim. We swim in the relationship (response) that our video provides. The feelings and thoughts that are provided as a reaction to the video. The swirling, complex emotional pool created between ourselves (character) and the memories/thoughts (video)

Swim Deep. To go deeper into our experience. When we swim deep, we force ourselves (and the audience) to confront the life of our character. The character's life and experience doesn't end when the scene ends. "It's uncomfortable down there (deep) There's no air. Bring the audience down there with you. Let them up for air now and then (release) but then, deep again." Don't swim fast, swim deep.

Task. A way to productively employ our Actor Brain. You'll note that when an actor is focused on a task (abrupt and often, isn't this fun, etc.) it allows the character to flow because the Actor Brain is productively employed. The actor will not have time for typical Actor Brain thoughts (nerves, judgement, self conscious, stiff, succeeding, etc.)

Tension/Release. Tension is present in every satisfying audience experience. That is why they lean forward, want to know what happens next, root for your character, cry at the end, etc. The tension is between you (the character, performance, story) and the audience. Tension has limits. Release is necessary. In release, the audience laughs, cheers, amens. The (continuous and instinctual) creating and releasing of tension. Discomfort.

Truth. We can create a truth for ourselves when we see what the character sees and let the lines become a reaction to what we are seeing. Note: Visuals always precede the words. Visuals are where words come from.

Un-presentability. Part of Anti-Acting. Helps actors present characters who "don't know they are being watched." A great illusion. To be Unpresentable gives the audience an "intimate" look at your character.

Unreasonableness. Heightened dramatic action. The reasonable response has no dramatic power. Many characters are based entirely on unreasonableness. (The Office) If these characters were reasonable, there would not even be a show. Unreasonableness provides longer dramatic arrows... greater impact.

Words. Words are not truth. They are the runoff, residual, by-product of truth. Words are selected through the video. The video is first, and the word is a response to the video. Inherently imperfect.

Duane Daniels is an actor, director, producer and coach. In television, Duane is most remembered for his role in the critically acclaimed TV series (and film) *Veronica Mars* starring Kristen Bell, and also appeared in *Big Shots, Invisible Man, The Chronicle, Fashion House* and *Tremors - the Series*.

He began acting on stage as a kid in Cleveland, Ohio. His early focus was on musical theatre and Duane gained a great deal of experience as a singer and dancer. For a few years, Duane was an opera singer. He has played most of the bass-baritone bad guys including playing the title role in Stephen Sondheim's *Sweeney Todd; The Demon Barber of Fleet Street* three times. As a physical comedian, Duane has logged over 2000 performances in *Triple Espresso; A Highly Caffeinated Comedy* in venues from San Diego to Dublin. Duane was Founder and Artistic Director of The Fritz Theatre in San Diego and ran the company for 18 years. During his tenure there, The Fritz produced over 200 plays, half of them premieres. He then was Artistic Director of Buzzworks Theatre in L.A. and Space 55 in Phoenix. Duane produced several premiers in New York and directed at the famed La MaMa

 Experimental Theatre, The Second City in Hollywood and The Old Globe Theatre in San Diego. Duane runs The Actor's WorkHouse in Phoenix and spends his summers teaching those methods at Berridge Programs in Normandy, France. He has won the Drama-Logue, ACT, Patte, Blitz, AriZoni and been nominated for the L.A Critics Association, LA Weekly and Garland (Variety Magazine) Awards.

Duane's musical *Home Town (Country Blue Saloon)* co-written with Margo Brookover, Jennifer Jones Nesbit and his brother Randy Daniels has won awards in early productions. He is currently developing a musical *Teenagers From Space* with co-writers Ron Foligno, Dennis Frederick and Lee Quarrie with music by Michael Sweeney and the L.A. band Alright Alright. Support Duane's projects at patreon.com/DuaneDaniels. actorsworkhouse@gmail.com.

Made in the USA
Columbia, SC
05 June 2019